FARMER
TO FATHER

*Finding God in
people, places and events*

Fr. Louis Studer, O.M.I.

Published by the Missionary Oblates of Mary Immaculate
9480 North De Mazenod Drive
Belleville, Illinois, 62223

Printed in the USA, by Bang Printing of Brainerd, MN

Dedication

I dedicate this book to my deceased parents for their loving guidance, example and patience, to my brothers and sisters for their care and support, to my friends for their encouragement and kindness, but, most especially, I dedicate this book to all those who continue to help make possible the ministry of the Missionary Oblates of Mary Immaculate through their generosity and prayers.

All of you have strengthened me in my vocation. I continue to remember you in my Mass intentions and prayers.

You are missionaries with the Oblates because you share in the good work we do. You help make it possible. We are very grateful to you.

Acknowledgements

First and foremost, I thank my good parents, whose patient example and life of prayer helped lead me to the Oblates and to the priesthood. I thank my brothers and sisters, June, Carolyn, Suzanne, David, Muriel and Elmer, whose love and care have sustained me in my vocation. I enjoy getting together with you.

I am privileged to be a member of the Missionary Oblates of Mary Immaculate. I admire the missionary work we do all over the world and the compassion and love, especially for the poor, with which we do that work. Somehow we usually manage to make it seem like fun. I admire that spirit.

I am likewise blessed to have many friends. You show your kindness with your reminders to take care of myself, not to worry so much, to keep busy and other parental micromanaging. Along with my brothers and sisters and Oblate friends, I love you for your advice, though I may sometimes forget to tell you or show it.

Thanks much as well to all the people with whom I have had the privilege to minister over the years in many different places and situations.

I acknowledge with special gratitude all my co-workers at the Missionary Association of Mary Immaculate and at the National Shrine of Our Lady of the Snows. You are valued for the good work you do, for your time and energy and for being missionaries with the Oblates. You are an extension of the missionary work of the Oblates in your own lives.

I also am grateful to Betty Lyke and June McGeehon for their patience and understanding and helpful suggestions with this manuscript but also with many other areas of my ministry at the Shrine and at the Missionary Association. I appreciate the fact that, as my Administrative Assistants, they always strive to make me look good. I know that is not always an easy task.

I also want to extend a special thanks to my co-workers who helped me with all the final stages of publishing this book. Thanks to our Writers, Annie Kessler and Bernadette McCaffrey, and to our Administrative Assistant, Kim Weilmuenster, for helping to "fine tune" and edit. Many thanks to Stacy Dambacher, Production Control Supervisor, who worked so diligently to iron out the details needed to publish this book. Thanks to our Designers, Sarah Abbott, Jamie Green and Allison Salzman, for their wonderful work in design and layout. Thanks to Bill Magrath, our Creative Supervisor, for overseeing the whole process. Tom Mulhall, Marketing Manager of the National Shrine of Our Lady of the Snows, and Cindy Streif, Donor Service Supervisor, were a great help as well. Associate Director of the Missionary Association of Mary Immaculate, Steve Piantanida, I thank you for your guidance and advice.

I'd also like to thank the Charitable Gifts Department with whom I work very closely. Especially, Lucille Green, Jack Weck, Rosalee Cavataio, Steve Wilmes, Dave Garris and Geri Moore; I enjoy working with you all.

A very special thanks to Tom Foppe of *Foppe DeSigns* for helping me with the title, designing the cover and for creating the wonderful art illustrations.

Most especially, however, I thank the donors to the Missionary Oblates. It is you, through your generosity, who make the ministry of 4,500 Oblate priests and Brothers in 70 countries of the world possible. Thank you for your prayers and for your goodwill. The poor of this world, helped by the Oblates, are grateful to you as well. Truly, you are partners with the Missionary Oblates.

May God bless all of you, your families and your loved ones. The Missionary Oblates remember you and pray for you each day.

Table of Contents

Introduction

The idea for this book grew out of some of the retreat conferences I have presented to various groups over the past several years as well as some reflection about the people and events that helped shape my life.

The underlying premise and theme of any retreat I have presented is that God is always present and active in our lives. At certain key points in our lives, such as when we were making a life altering decision or facing a serious crisis, we may have been in touch with that Presence in a more profound, intense way. But it is inconceivable that a God of total love and goodness would not always be active and present in our lives at every moment, in season and out of season.

So often we lose touch with what God is doing and saying in our lives. We forget or fail to renew and refresh that relationship and re-discover what God is saying and doing. We don't keep our end of the Covenant, of the relationship. Only at certain key moments, such as a retreat or a crisis, do we seriously ask and consider where God is in our lives, what He is doing and saying.

I believe that God sometimes reveals Himself to us most clearly in the ordinary events and circumstances of our lives. He uses these events to show us His love, to draw us closer to Himself. Too often we fail to reflect on those seemingly ordinary circumstances to discern His deeper message of love and care for us.

The purpose of this book is to encourage the reader to take a closer look back at his or her life and re-discover and renew how God has been present in the people and events that have helped shape us. For me, this is prayer at its richest.

Biblical scholars have pointed out that it is precisely this kind of prayer that Jesus would have used in His own life, for instance, at the time of Passover. At this Passover (Last Supper) meal, the devout Jew would typically recall the great events of how God had acted on behalf of his nation and race. He would recall how God had delivered them as a people out of the slavery of Egypt, had led them to the land of promise, had raised up great religious and political leaders — judges and prophets, kings and rulers, to serve them. Then, the religious Jew would recall how that same God reveals Himself in his own personal life, in and through the daily events and relationships of that life.

Just like the fisherman who loves to tell the story about the size of the fish he caught and to further exaggerate the size of that fish every time he tells the story, so too as we recall these events of our lives, the events and people and God's acting on our behalf becomes a deeper part of who we are. We continue to teach ourselves again and again about a God who is continually acting on our behalf because of His tremendously intense love for us, each time we recall the events.

For me, recalling and renewing and reliving some of these moments and carefully discerning God's message and purpose in these people and events helps make God more personal, more real and more loving. We can then prepare ourselves to better discover His presence and action in our lives, not only in the present, but in the past and in the future as well.

Chapter One:
Iowa: A Place to Grow

In the 1970s, the state of Iowa used a marketing slogan to bring vacationers and entrepreneurs to this beautiful part of the United States. The campaign certainly grabbed the attention and interest of many because of its unique message. How successful it was in its goal, I'm not sure. The slogan was simple and to the point which was part of the reason for the attention it got. The signs read, "Iowa: A Place to Grow."

The ads captured my attention because I couldn't have disagreed with them more! I could understand how for some people the state of Iowa was a safe, healthy environment in which to raise children. On one of the many gorgeous, sprawling farms in Iowa young people can learn the value of a hard day's work, enjoy the clean air of the open spaces, eat beef, pork or chicken raised on that same farm and, of course, munch down on freshly picked sweet corn, Iowa's signature product.

Although Iowa boasts about its many midsize urban areas, the state is still considered largely rural.

It was on one of these beautiful, sprawling farms in the north central part of the state that I was born and raised.

I hated being raised on a farm!

The deep, rich, black soil, perfect for growing corn and soybeans, meant nothing to me. The fact that our farm was able to provide fresh beef, pork or chicken for our dining pleasure each day, not to mention the potatoes, lettuce and sweet corn from the garden, was lost on me. To me, farming meant work that I didn't like to do.

My parents were successful farmers. They worked hard and loved showing us seven children the value of work! Each one of us had our own chores to do and, for all of us, summers were spent hoeing weeds out of the corn and soybean fields.

I was certainly not one of the children who contributed to my parents' success as farmers.

One of my farm chores each evening was to collect the eggs in our chicken house. This chicken house was the place on the farm where my brothers, sisters and I tried to spend as little time as possible. It was dusty and dirty, made worse by the fact that the chickens would rustle up the dust as they crazily flew from one end of the building to the other.

This chore might not have been too severe were it not for the fact that the chickens were usually nesting on the eggs when I wanted to collect them.

I was instructed by dad to gently reach under the chicken and gather the eggs so as not to disturb the chickens. Every time I tried this approach, however, the chicken would peck my hand. I knew that somehow I had to retrieve those eggs. The solution? Pull the chicken off the eggs (grabbing it by the wing was the most convenient method for me), throw it out of the way and then gather the eggs.

A couple weeks later after I began this chore, dad announced at supper that he couldn't figure out why the chickens weren't laying more eggs. Later, of course, he discovered why. I think this incident, along with many others on the farm, caused him to begin to wonder, "Will I have to support him all my life?"

I found ways to avoid farm work with an incredibly active imagination.

Hoeing weeds out of the corn and bean fields proved to be quite a boring task. Dad found a small hoe for me, perfect for a smaller child. I quickly recognized that my hoe was smaller than my older brother's and sisters' hoes. Hiding this instrument of labor would render it impossible for me to continue this arduous labor, I reasoned. So, I hid my hoe in our grove behind a large tree. My reasoning, of course, was that no one would ever find my hoe in the grove, as no one ever went there.

Dad was understandably miffed, when I announced that the hoe was inexplicably lost. Completely undaunted, he went to town the next day and purchased a hoe, sawed off part of the handle, and instructed me to try to remember more carefully where I put my hoe so I wouldn't lose it again.

So much for my creative ingenuity. I don't know whatever happened to the hoe I left in the grove. Dad may have discovered it years later. I hope he smiled when he found it!

I have often thought that, if it were not for a television program called "Bart's Clubhouse," I might have become at least a mediocre farmer one day.

"Bart's Clubhouse" aired each afternoon at 5:00 p.m., chore time in Iowa, and featured cartoons as well as Bart's own scientific inventions and experiments. He explained why water freezes in cold weather, why pouring hot water on ice to remove the ice from the steps of one's home is not a smart idea. (I didn't believe Bart and tried it once, much to my father's dismay.) I learned plenty every afternoon from Bart.

One of my chores was to turn on the water faucet to fill the cow tank. I was usually rather faithful in turning the water on but then often became so engrossed in Bart's latest scientific experiment, or a new cartoon, that I would forget to run the quarter mile from the house to turn off the water. The result, of course, was a huge mud puddle around the tank. That meant having to wear rubber boots to get near the tank, a task that my dad and brothers, David and Elmer, didn't relish.

Dad had given me several warnings about not letting the tank run over. His warnings usually went in one ear and out the other. Sometimes, while watching "Bart's Clubhouse," I would remember that the tank was probably ready to run over but, not wanting to miss a single minute of the show, would wait until a commercial to shut off the water.

Despite his patience, dad realized that his repeated warnings were going unheeded. And soon thereafter the first of the spankings began.

"Louis, find me a stick," was the clear message that I was soon to receive a spanking. Not only would I receive a spanking, I even had to find the stick with which I would be spanked. Despite the spankings, none of which was ever harsh or unjust, I continued to let the tank run over. Even as I got older I would sometimes wait for the commercial before running the quarter mile to turn off the water. If Bart hadn't worked so hard at his scientific experiments, I might have become a more conscientious farmer. But somehow I doubt it!

Even worse than letting the cow tank run over was the night I was given the responsibility to complete all the chores myself. Essentially, that meant watering and feeding the cows, pigs and chickens. And, of course, gathering the eggs. I'm not sure what condition the chickens were in at this point, or even if they were still laying eggs! Mom and dad were successful farmers, but that never included our egg business.

On the evening I had responsibility for doing all the chores, instead of getting an early start, I procrastinated; perhaps out of fear, perhaps out of laziness, perhaps a little of both.

I began watching "Bart's Clubhouse" and told

myself that dad and David wouldn't be home until late and I had plenty of time to get the chores done.

It was summer and I knew it would be light outside until almost ten o'clock. They were at my grandpa's farm, baling hay.

I continued to watch program after program, telling myself after each one that I would soon begin the chores.

At about 9:15 p.m. I heard the distinct sound of the putt-putt of our John Deere tractor and knew that dad and David were home. I hadn't lifted a hand to do any of the chores that dad had so carefully instructed me about and showed me how to do. I hadn't even turned on the water this night to fill the cow tank. As I heard dad's footsteps getting closer to the living room where I continued to watch TV, I reasoned that, at least tonight, I wouldn't get a spanking because I hadn't let the cow tank run over!

Dad stood at the edge of the living room and innocently asked, "How did the chores go?"

"I wasn't able to finish them," I muttered.

"Why not?" he asked sternly.

"I wasn't sure how to start them," I quietly and very politely answered.

"I thought you understood yesterday..." and he stopped.

I looked at his dirty, sweaty face and noticed a few bits of hay had stuck to the sweat there. He stared at me for what seemed a long time. So quietly that I almost didn't hear him, he said, "I'll do the chores myself."

In that moment I knew I had greatly disappointed

my dad. I wanted him to punish me. I knew he wouldn't yell at me; neither mom nor dad raised their voices to us kids. But no spanking this time? For just a short moment, I wondered if I hadn't gotten a spanking because I hadn't let the cow tank run over! But quickly I decided that this time dad had a deeper message to teach me. It taught me a lot about his deep disappointment in me.

Besides hiding my hoe to avoid some labor on the farm, another favorite tactic of mine was staying at my grandmother's house in the summer. If summer days at home meant hoeing weeds, summer days at grandma's house meant playing dominoes. What fun we had!

She allowed, even encouraged me, to eat whatever foods I liked when I stayed with her. She tried to make sure that whatever foods I wanted were prepared exactly to my taste.

One summer afternoon, after several games of dominoes at which I usually won (I'm sure she often let me win), she asked me if I wanted some Kool-Aid.

"And what kind would you like?" she kindly offered.

I think she stocked more flavors of Kool-Aid than the grocery store itself so I was relatively sure she would have whatever flavor I wanted.

"How about root beer?" I suggested.

"Root beer it is," she affirmed. She quickly made the customary package of two quarts of Kool-Aid and asked me how I liked it.

I took a second sip, just to be sure my taste buds weren't playing tricks on me.

"Grandma, it tastes kind of sweet."

"Too sweet?" she immediately wanted to know.

"Yes, too sweet."

She grabbed the large pitcher of Kool-Aid, poured what remained in my glass into the pitcher, kicked open the screen door and threw the contents of the pitcher onto the front lawn. She did all this in one grand, sweeping action.

"We'll make another pitcher of root beer Kool-Aid and see if we can't do better the second time."

The second batch was perfect.

Staying with her definitely beat hoeing thistles and throwing chickens!

Grandma's care, mom's understanding and dad's patience certainly taught me, at a tender age, the meaning of love and compassion but, unfortunately, not the value of farming!

In seventh grade, an Oblate priest by the name of Fr. John Frischmon visited our grade school in Wesley. He spoke to the seventh and eighth grades about becoming a priest or a religious Brother or Sister. He then spoke separately to the boys about joining the Missionary Oblates of Mary Immaculate, a Catholic community of missionary priests and Brothers. Father John explained that, if interested, we would study at Our Lady of the Ozarks High School Seminary in Carthage, Missouri, after completing eighth grade. I was somewhat interested but knew I had to wait another year and a half before I would go to Carthage. I never said anything to mom or dad about Fr. John's visit, wanting to give more time to my decision on my own.

I did tell Fr. John that I was somewhat interested

14

and even surprised myself when I suddenly blurted out that it might be worth his while to come back the next year to talk to me. He promised me he would return the next year.

Almost to the day, one year later, he returned to St. Joseph's. He talked about religious vocations in a general way, as he had the year before, but there was a greater urgency in his voice to speak to the seventh and eighth grade boys.

He wanted a show of hands among the eighth grade boys, indicating who of us was thinking about studying at Our Lady of the Ozarks Seminary that fall. I reluctantly raised my hand, fearing that I might be the only one. I looked around and quickly saw that what I suspected was true. No one else showed any interest. Father John announced to everyone that he would speak with me and my parents that evening. After his talk, I spoke privately with him.

"Would you like to come for supper?" I bashfully asked.

"That would be great!" he answered, much too quickly I thought.

Mom had arrived at school to drive us kids home, shortly after I finished my meeting with Fr. Frischmon. I was the last one to get into the car.

"Guess what, mom?" I excitedly asked.

With all the chatter in the car, I don't think she heard me. So I continued on, relatively sure that I would get her attention with what I was about to say.

"Mom, there was a missionary priest at our school today and I invited him over for supper."

Raising seven children made my mom an expert at preparing meals, big and small alike. Her respect and esteem for priests and Religious, however, caused her some concern about what she would serve for supper that evening.

"And all I have thawed out is hamburger," she said.

Mom didn't feel quite so bad after Fr. John ate three hamburgers in quick succession at supper and a large bowl of ice cream after!

Father John spent the evening talking to my parents about the program at Our Lady of the Ozarks Seminary. Both mom and dad asked Fr. John a lot of questions about my traveling five hundred miles from home, at thirteen years of age, to consider a vocation to the Oblates and to the priesthood.

I think dad was relieved that I now might not attempt to farm and thereby become a complete failure. And mom wisely told me, in Fr. John's presence, that she and dad would make me promise to stay at the seminary at least until Christmas.

At the time, I couldn't realize how difficult, or how wise on her part, that promise would prove to become.

As I look back on my decision, I realize that Our Lady of the Ozarks Seminary was attractive to me for much the same reason that staying with my grandma was: I would be away from the farm! The lessons of goodness and compassion, shown to me by my parents and my grandma, and the many ways I discovered God working in my life through the Oblate priests and Brothers at Carthage were blessings I would never forget. Being away from home at thirteen also taught me a lot about an appreciation for the state of Iowa. I learned the values of living on a farm, the generosity of my parents in allowing me to pursue a clouded dream and the fun and kindness of my brothers and sisters.

At the time, I didn't really make a conscious choice for the Oblates. I chose the seminary because of a possible vocation but mainly, I think, to get off the farm.

Mom and dad drove me to Carthage the Saturday of Labor Day weekend. We arrived in the late afternoon, enjoyed a delicious dinner of southern fried chicken at one of Carthage's finest restaurants and stayed at a hotel near the seminary.

They left Carthage after Mass and lunch at the seminary the following afternoon. As their car pulled out of the seminary driveway, I felt a sinking, funny sensation in my stomach, sort of like hunger pangs yet I knew I wasn't hungry in the least. That feeling was to stay with me for what seemed like a very long time.

Chapter Two:
Meeting the Oblates

As my parents' car drove out of the seminary driveway and that sinking feeling in my stomach grew stronger, my first thought was to get busy. I had all this unpacking to do and besides, classes would be starting already Tuesday morning.

I must have told myself that I didn't have much time to get all my clothes, bedding, toiletries and school supplies in their proper places before Tuesday morning. In fact, I had two full days to accomplish this simple task. I knew that once classes started I would be very busy. Father Frischmon had told me the seminary schedule would keep me from getting bored!

I finished getting everything in order in about two hours. I looked at my watch: 3:00 p.m.

There were some activities planned to keep the

students busy, especially the new guys. But baseball or volleyball or checkers or ping pong didn't sound like much fun, especially when I didn't know any of the other students. And that sinking, funny feeling moving more deeply into the pit of my stomach was getting worse.

I didn't even recognize at the time that I was getting homesick. Never having experienced it before, I didn't know what it was.

Staying at grandma's house for three weeks at a time during the summer caused me to believe that homesickness would never be a problem for me.

I was reluctant to talk to anyone at the seminary.

The loneliness I felt was new and strange for me. I felt tears welling up inside throughout the afternoon. Just before supper, I went into the bathroom, closed the stall door and cried. All I could think about were the faces of mom and dad and my brothers and sisters. I seemed to know this was making my situation worse but I couldn't help myself. The more I thought about each one of them, the more I cried and a vicious cycle began which was to last, to some degree, for almost two months.

I didn't go to supper that Sunday evening. I didn't go to the movie in the auditorium after supper. I stayed in the bathroom stall and wept. It felt good to cry, to continue to think about my family, to wallow in my self pity, but I knew that I was only making my situation worse. I went to bed early, before the other students came to the dormitory after night prayer, and cried myself to sleep.

The next day, Labor Day, was worse. It was easy to

spend time alone since there were no formally organized activities and I reasoned that no one probably knew which students had yet arrived.

After Mass and breakfast, I went up to the dormitory under the pretense of finishing some unpacking but really it was to occupy the bathroom stall and find a quiet place to cry.

That was how I spent Labor Day. I skipped dinner and supper, the movie that night and evening prayers. I went to the dormitory before the other students did and cried.

Tuesday was different. We were awakened at 6:20 a.m. and were kept busy every minute of the day. Prayer, Mass, classes, meals, sports activities, two evening study halls and night prayer filled the day. We were told that during the second evening study hall we should write a letter to our parents, telling them how we were doing and about the activities which occupied our time at the seminary.

My letter read:

"Dear Mom and Dad, I don't like this place. I never wanted to be a priest. I want to come home. Send money for a bus ticket right away. I'll see you soon. Love, Louis."

They probably received my letter that Friday. Mom must have written that very day because I received a response the following Tuesday. I couldn't figure out what was taking so long for her to get back to me, but as I look back now I realize she responded as quickly as she possibly could.

She wrote:

"Dear Louis, I'm sorry you're not adjusting better to

the seminary. You promised dad and me that you would stay until Christmas. We will keep you to that promise. Love, Mom."

Having spent yet another miserable weekend of homesickness in the bathroom stall, I crushed the letter, threw it in the wastebasket and, after afternoon classes, cried in the bathroom stall until late afternoon study hall.

I knew that I couldn't skip seminary activities anymore. Attendance at all seminary activities was required. I still cried myself to sleep each night. I refused to talk to anyone about my homesickness because I couldn't imagine that it would do any good. No one would be able to help me with the mess I was in, I reasoned.

Now, when I thought about my family, I tried to avoid thinking about mom. How could she treat me this way, I wondered. Being angry with her only made my homesickness seem worse.

As I look back, I realize how wise she was. Obviously, she knew that a part of my desire to go to the seminary was to leave the farm, but I'm sure she also saw in me some desire for the Oblates and the priesthood.

It was that desire that gave her the strength to make me keep my promise. She was wise beyond her years, not to mention that she was of sufficient strength not to give in to the easy route for both her and me. It must have been very difficult for her to tell me "no."

On my continuing path to the priesthood, I often thought of her resolve, her strength of character, especially in my difficult moments of decision, and it was often her example that helped me weather whatever crisis I was experiencing at the time.

As time passed and we became busier with classes, homework, sports, manual labor responsibilities and spiritual activities; my homesickness gradually took a backseat. I still sometimes cried at night, but as I began to make friends, much of the homesickness subsided.

My parents surprised me with a visit to the seminary on November 1st. Mom may have thought that I really didn't love her anymore and that a visit was necessary to rekindle that bond. Besides, I'm sure by then my letters were more positive in spirit and she realized that a visit wouldn't uproot my resolve to stay. It was still with some difficulty that I waved goodbye to them a couple days later. As I resumed the regular activities of each day and realized I'd be home for Christmas in a short five weeks, I was soon fine again.

At Christmas, I was re-introduced quickly to the farm, to the chores, to the cold Iowa winters.

I had forgotten the terrible chore of carrying pails of water to the chickens through the snow. If that doesn't sound bad enough, imagine how the water splashes on your pant leg, and then quickly freezes in this process. There's that problem, plus the uneven footing of walking in the heavy snow. Seminary was looking better and better as each day of vacation passed.

I boarded the bus back to Our Lady of the Ozarks Seminary on January 2nd, having enjoyed my vacation at home but happy also to see friends again at the seminary.

Homesickness was definitely behind me. I wasn't sure about wanting to become an Oblate, or even a priest; but I certainly knew I didn't want to be a farmer, especially not in the cold winters of Iowa! Most especially, not if dad continued to keep chickens on the farm!

As I continued on through the seminary in high school and college, I began to realize how the Oblates, Brothers and priests alike, were unique.

Being from a diocesan parish in northern Iowa, I imagined that all priests were pastors of parishes, like the priests I knew before entering the seminary. While I thought parish ministry was attractive, I also knew that some Brothers, Sisters and priests taught in high schools and colleges.

I thought I would enjoy teaching. Many of the Oblates who taught me at Our Lady of the Ozarks Seminary and at Lewis University where I attended college seminary were excellent teachers. In fact, after the college preparatory classes at Our Lady of the Ozarks Seminary, college academics seemed quite easy. Typically, the Oblates were well prepared in both their teaching and their preaching. I also learned that the Oblates were in many different countries of the world. They lived in community to support and strengthen one another in their ministries; their activities were many and varied, depending on the needs of the people in a particular place.

While walking through the corn and bean fields of Iowa as a youngster, I would often wonder to myself: would I ever be able to get off the farm? Would I ever get to some far away place like Des Moines? Chicago seemed much too far away to even think seriously about.

I wanted to see the gold dome of the State Capitol building in Des Moines. Would I die without ever seeing the Lincoln Memorial? I wondered. And these Oblates are ministering all over the world. In fact, the Oblates like to say of themselves, "The Oblate Cross Covers the World." That was exciting, invigorating news for me!

As a youngster, our family would gather each evening to pray the rosary together. I usually dreaded it, but a few swats on the backside quickly taught me that mom and dad were serious about this time of prayer together as a family.

I remember mom and dad praying their morning prayers together in the dining room as we were preparing to go to school in the morning. Their devotion to prayer and to the Blessed Mother was exemplary.

Mom and dad always seemed rather reserved around priests and Religious. I'm not sure if it was the times, or if their respect of priests and Religious caused them to treat these spiritual leaders with deference.

I soon noticed that with the Oblates, mom and dad seemed more at ease. So much so that mom once confessed to me, "Oh, being around the Oblates is just different. They're so friendly and open."

She, along with my oldest sister, June, whose sentiment was similar to mom and dad's, would even tease the Oblates about their weight or age. I was amazed how familiar they could be with priests and Religious.

Throughout my thirteen years of preparation for the Oblate way of life and priesthood, I got to know many of my peers well. Some of my fellow classmates would complain to me that their parents were often asking them how sure they were that this was their vocation. They said this happened especially during the summer, asking whether they were returning to the seminary in the fall.

I never experienced that kind of pressure from my parents. Although I was pretty sure that my parents and my family would be proud to have a Religious in the family, neither mom nor dad ever once asked me whether I was going back to the seminary. I felt a healthy freedom to make my own choice. My sisters, June, Carolyn, Suzanne and Muriel, only said they would never call me "Father" after ordination. So much for their loving support!

The Missionary Oblates of Mary Immaculate were becoming a good fit for me. Their varied and numerous ministries on six continents of the world and their strong devotion to Mary under the title of Mary Immaculate as well as the support they gave to each other in community all fit in well with what I knew to be important to me in religious life.

Living on a farm four miles from my classmates in grade school meant that I got to know my parents, brothers and sisters well. Working with my brothers and sisters in the corn and bean fields, feeding the animals, praying the rosary together, playing baseball together — all of these things helped me appreciate and learn about the support I would need in religious life. These experiences helped me grow closer with my community members, other Oblates committed to the charism of St. Eugene De Mazenod, the Founder. The opportunity to become involved in a wide variety of ministries, to minister in many cultures and countries, to further my devotion to the Blessed Mother, all became signs that the Missionary Oblates were the community that I wanted to join. The Spirit was showing me, leading and guiding me, to this missionary community. It seemed to me that if I was to decide on a vocation to religious life, the Missionary Oblates could fulfill the dreams, desires and values of my youth. Besides, I would be off the farm forever!

Throughout my youth, I had remembered a worried look on my dad's face from early May until the end of October. In Iowa, this is the growing season. Too much rain or wind or snow or hail or heat or insects can wipe out the farmer's profits in a very short time. So, from the time the seed is placed in the ground in early May until the crop is in the storage bins in late October, a possible disaster looms heavily in the mind of the farmer.

Mom and dad were well aware of the need of God in their lives. I thought often about dad's worried look during the growing season as I pondered my own choice; my decision to become a Religious, a priest, a Missionary Oblate of Mary Immaculate.

I could easily identify with dad's radical dependency on God for a rich and bountiful harvest and his worried, concerned look until the harvest was in the storage bins. That concern and worry became my own as I struggled to decide what direction and decision I should definitively give my life.

The very early years.

This picture, and others that I ruined, is from my oldest sister's and brother-in-law's wedding.

My brother David and I served Mass for Fr. Lawrence Klein, Pastor of St. Joseph's Parish, Wesley, Iowa.

Fr. John Frischmon, O.M.I., visited my grade school and invited me to the high school seminary in Carthage, Missouri.

My mom and dad were always supportive of my vocation to the Oblates and priesthood.

The first formal family portrait.
Back row, left to right: Louis, June, Muriel, Suzanne, Carolyn, David
Front row, left to right: Mom, Elmer, Dad

Sr. Mary Vincent, O.S.F., Milwaukee Franciscan, who taught me in 4th, 5th, and 6th grades.

The chapel at Our Lady of the Ozarks Seminary offered me a lot of consolation in time of homesickness.

With my 2nd grade teacher, Sr. Mary Lenore, O.S.F., Milwaukee Franciscan.

With Aaron Jelinek at the Oblates'
Novitiate in Godfrey, Illinois. This was my
most difficult year of seminary.

With some of the students at St. Henry's
Seminary. I enjoyed teaching more than
I thought I would.

Chapter Three:
The Vowed Life

T he ancient Israelites believed that God directly controlled all the circumstances and events of their lives. Everything that happened to them was the direct intervention and action of God in their lives.

When their crops were bountiful it was because God was rewarding them for their goodness, for their adherence to His law. When they lost a battle or war, they believed it was because they had sinned and God was punishing them. While few people in modern society would believe that God acts so directly in our lives, the radical dependency of the Israelites on the might and power of God in their lives is an important theological concept and one that helped them to continue to depend on God always.

My experience is that there are few people who cannot recall an event in their lives when they believe that God directly intervened on their behalf. It might have been a lesson to be learned, a relationship to be healed, a person to be forgiven or a principle of faith to be understood. For Christians and Catholics to affirm belief in a God who loves us as His people, it makes no sense for us not to then also affirm that this God of love is constantly acting on our behalf.

The poster that was popular in the 1960s rightly affirmed: "God is a verb, not a noun."

God is present and active in each one of our lives. Our challenge is to discern what He is saying and doing at any given moment and, indeed, in all moments of our lives.

Scripture speaks of this action of God on our behalf in interesting ways. The prophet Ezekiel finds God in the whisper; Jacob discovers Him in a dream. His presence is likewise discerned in the wind, as the Spirit. This is the marvelous experience of those early followers of Jesus, gathered together in the upper room on Pentecost. This force of wind, the Spirit, strengthens them to go out and preach the Good News fearlessly.

Each one of these images can be very powerful, but each one is also elusive, ephemeral, difficult to get a handle on.

These three images say so much about who God is and how He acts in our lives.

There can be no question about God's capability to

be a powerful force in our lives and in our world. My own experience of God's presence to me in prayer has, at times, been overwhelming. At other times, He seems far away and unapproachable.

Why isn't God always close to us, approachable and present? I think it's because God respects our freedom, at all costs. The images of the wind, the whisper and the dream speak about a God who we cannot capture, confine or contain. God will remain God at all costs.

Sometimes, we may wish that God would hit us over the head with an iron skillet so we would know for sure what action to take in a given moment. But then God would be interfering in our freedom to choose. I believe that for God to treat us in such a manner is unthinkable for Him.

More than anything, besides His desire to have us with Him in paradise forever, is God's insistence that we are a free people to choose for or against Him. He wants to be in relationship with us and that means we must freely choose to love Him, as He does us. Without this ability to choose freely, a real loving relationship with God, or with anyone else, is not possible. God profoundly understands this, even if we ourselves might sometimes find it difficult to understand or accept.

Can we imagine a world in which there is no sin, and no suffering? We are undoubtedly tempted to say "yes," but no suffering and sin also implies a world in which there is no choice, no decision and no true, lasting love. It would be a cold, apathetic world with no possibility for love, either.

Jesus was given this freedom to choose whether or not to follow the Father's will.

We are each given this same freedom to choose for or against God and one another, and even ourselves. The freedom, of course, means bad choices are possible and the consequences are sometimes sin, suffering and pain for us and for others. But the loving, lasting relationship must mean that the two persons have freely chosen each other out of love and respect. God seems to understand this profoundly.

In choosing the vowed religious life, I recognized the value of giving myself to the vows of poverty, chastity and obedience. The Missionary Oblates also profess a fourth vow of perseverance.

For me, these four vows directly militate against the values of a culture that is mired in material possessions, has a lack of respect for one another as unique, valued persons, and lacks the value of listening to God and remaining faithful to Him and to one another.

As I prepared to profess these vows of poverty, chastity, obedience and perseverance as a Missionary Oblate of Mary Immaculate, I tried to summarize in a practical way how I would try to live these vows in my daily life. Each vow seemed to address itself to some "do's" and "don'ts."

Poverty — trusting that my religious community will provide for me;

- allowing others to have some control over my time and energy;

- allowing others, especially other members of the community, to use my possessions;

- freely admitting that I don't know all the answers or have all the answers to life's questions;

- acknowledging that I don't have my life completely together or in order;

- realizing that I need to learn from others, even sometimes learn from them some truths about myself.

Chastity — not becoming possessed by any one person and allowing many people to enter my life;

- making sure I have close friends whom I can trust and from whom I can get good advice about important personal issues;

- being free enough with my life that I am approachable and available to others most of the time.

Obedience — in dialogue with good friends and with my religious superiors I discover my life's ministry;

- learning my strengths and gifts and realizing that I must use them for the good of the community;

- recognizing that living in community is almost always preferable to living on my own;

- opening myself to what others say to me and how they perceive me.

Perseverance — a promise to remain faithful to discerning God's presence and action in my life, what He is asking of me, what He is doing for me, how He continues to gift me. Perseverance also means faithfulness to my friends and loved ones whenever they need me or ask me for help, and faithfulness to prayer each day to deepen my relationship and love for the Lord.

When I first heard that Oblates professed a vow of perseverance, I quickly dismissed its importance by saying it was simply our Founder's way of reminding his Oblates that they were to live the vows of poverty, chastity and obedience for life, to persevere to the end, so to speak. Now, I see that vow of perseverance as the one that unites the other three — a fidelity to God's promises, a fidelity to relationship with others and a fidelity to oneself to grow in wisdom and grace, to grow in the vowed life.

Understanding the vows in this way helped me choose the Missionary Oblates and priesthood as the meaningful way to live my life. I vowed to live poverty, chastity, obedience and perseverance for life as a Missionary Oblate of Mary Immaculate on August 19, 1975, and was ordained to the priesthood in the beautiful Iowa town of my boyhood, Wesley, on June 19, 1976.

My training for priesthood was finished. I felt

adequately prepared to begin ministry and was anxious to leave the idyllic world of seminary life. I had much yet to learn. No one could have convinced me of that then, however.

Chapter Four:
Learning on the Job:
First Years in Ministry

My first assignment as an Oblate priest was as Associate Pastor of St. Patrick's Church in McCook, Nebraska. The Oblates had served this southwestern Nebraska town since 1908.

Previous to my arrival in McCook, a week after my ordination, I had never met Fr. Cyril Foppe, O.M.I., Pastor of the parish there. My brother David and niece Denise drove me to McCook and I dressed casually for the twelve hour, two day trip from Wesley. When I arrived at the rectory, I rang the doorbell and Fr. Foppe answered.

"And what can I do for you?" was his greeting.

He had no idea who I was. I was no more familiar with him.

The first weeks after my arrival I spent my days unpacking, celebrating daily Mass, sending thank you notes for ordination gifts and learning a few of the ropes of the parish.

I remember that my heart wasn't in the ministry of the parish much. It was July when the majority of events and activities shut down in a parish. Although I met many of the parishioners at the weekend Masses, I didn't get to know them well enough to feel comfortable socializing with them.

None of this mattered very much to me then because my thoughts were primarily focused on the vacation I would be taking with my brothers David and Elmer and my nephews Verne, Paul and Jerry in early August. The six of us were driving to California to attend a few of the Dodgers and the Angels baseball games and see the country.

We were out to prove that there could be no prettier or more productive state than Iowa.

The six of us were more than relatives; we were friends and somehow we all knew this would be the trip of a lifetime. My mind and heart were fixated on these two weeks of August during that entire first month in the parish.

The trip turned out to be more fun and adventuresome than any of us even imagined.

We rented a camper and hooked it to the back of a pickup truck and promised ourselves we would save some money by sleeping in the camper. There wasn't room for four of us, much less six and, after freezing in the camper the first night of the trip in the Rocky Mountains, we decided that a motel was a much better idea, even if a much more expensive one.

The trip turned out to be more expensive for another reason as well. While driving into Angels Stadium between two concrete pillars, we forgot that the windows on the side of the camper had been cranked open. In our hurry to get to the ballgame, the two windows were ripped off the camper by the unmovable pillars, as we anxiously drove into the ballpark.

There was no way this incident was going to ruin our trip. Unfortunately, the owner of the camper couldn't fully share our sense of humor when we returned the camper to him ten days later.

We drove from McCook to California and back to Iowa in eleven days. I wanted to spend a couple days with my parents and family in Iowa before returning to McCook. I was fully aware that in mid August there wouldn't be a lot of farm work to do so I felt relatively safe to go home!

My brother, David, offered to drive me back to McCook that following Saturday. He spent the evening with me at the rectory and needed to return to Iowa the next day.

Saturday night, as I was celebrating Mass for the people at St. Patrick's, I was sensing again, for the first time since my freshman year of high school, that funny, strange, empty feeling in the pit of my stomach. Sunday morning I felt even worse.

After the Masses and a quick lunch, my brother told me he needed to get on the road. We quickly said our goodbyes and I walked back into the empty rectory.

Both the pastor and the part-time associate pastor were gone on vacation. I knew I would be alone in the rectory for the next couple days.

I walked through the rectory, went upstairs to the bedrooms, back downstairs to the main level, then downstairs to the basement. I repeated this trek a few times and then suddenly ran out to the parish car and began driving through town to try to catch up to my brother's car. It was quite by sudden instinct that I did this, without thought.

What I would have said to my brother if I had caught up to him, I do not know. For some reason I felt I needed to reach him, talk to him, not let him leave me there alone. I wonder if I might have tried to convince him that I wanted to go back home with him.

That Sunday and the following week was very lonely. They were difficult days for me. I spent this time wondering if I hadn't made a mistake by becoming an Oblate and a priest. I celebrated Mass for the parishioners each day but wondered the whole time what I would do all day. I had no desire to get to know any of the parishioners.

I couldn't concentrate on my prayers. I ate little and for an Iowa farm boy, that is a first and most certain indication that the problem is serious.

I considered calling the Provincial to tell him that I had made a serious vocational mistake. I was afraid he would tell me that I had promised him I would stay until Christmas! (Maybe he had talked to my mom!)

I wasn't at all sure I could stay in McCook until Christmas, much less even stay an Oblate priest until Christmas!

There was no awareness, or care on my part, of what

the needs of the people in McCook might be or any desire to become acquainted with the town or the people. I didn't visit the hospital or any homes. I was barely able to write a few thank you notes for ordination gifts.

Writing thank you notes was the task I had set out to do the first day after the part-time Associate Pastor, Fr. Charlie Meyer, O.M.I., returned from vacation. After morning Mass, he bounded into my office to ask, "Have you ever been to Cheyenne?"

"Where's Cheyenne?" I wondered.

"Why, I believe it's in Wyoming."

"I mean, how far away is it?"

"A good five hours by car," he answered. "Rodeo days are on now and they're quite the thing to see," he continued. "You don't have rodeo days in Iowa, I'll bet."

"Oh, Charlie, not today, I don't think so," I answered, thinking I could get out of it.

"I'd sure appreciate it if you would go," he quickly responded. "I think you'd get quite a kick out of it."

We got to Cheyenne at 4:30 p.m., ate at the Holiday Inn restaurant, and began the five-hour drive back to McCook. We never got near the rodeo. We wouldn't have known rodeo days were happening except for the fact there was a banner strewn across the main street of Cheyenne, announcing the same.

On the trip, we talked about some of the Oblates Fr. Charlie had known and loved, the ministry assignments he had had, some Oblate foreign missions he had visited and about life in general. He even mentioned a few difficult, challenging moments in his life and how, with the wise counsel of a spiritual advisor, he had met those obstacles.

Father Charlie was a quick study. He had sensed my loneliness and fear and yes, homesickness. He knew a ten-hour road trip in which I would be trapped to listen to his sage advice might be a welcome beginning to invite me to at least try some ministry in McCook.

What I didn't know then was that this first year of priesthood would be one of the most difficult and loneliest of thirty-one years of ministry. I learned that commitments, whether to priesthood, or marriage, or religious life, or friendship aren't made once and forever. Commitments will last, and remain meaningful, only if we are willing to re-commit again and again. That was the primary lesson I learned that first year of priesthood; that, and I was also taught what forgiveness is all about.

I had quite a bit of work I needed to do to take me out of my self-centeredness and self-pity. The Oblates with whom I shared community that year — Fr. Cyril Foppe, Fr. Charlie Meyer, Brother Lon Konold — were most willing to help teach me how to minister, but I had to recognize some personal obstacles that were still in the way before I would be able to unselfishly give of myself to and for others.

I remember sharing with my spiritual advisor that year — I did take Fr. Meyer's advice — how after my sophomore year of high school I had chastised my mom for praying the rosary during Mass. I had learned in the high school seminary what constituted proper liturgical behavior during Mass, according to the documents of the Second Vatican Council. Mom faintly smiled when I corrected her but was secretly hurt, I think. Only later would I recognize my selfish need to show her my superior knowledge of the documents of the Second Vatican Council in which Catholics were encouraged to take an active role in the ritual of the Mass rather than in private devotions.

How I could cavalierly correct and admonish this holy, prayerful woman made me later realize the long road I must travel to become a servant to God's people.

My spiritual advisor was able to surface a valuable story from my earlier life during that year in McCook in which I came to realize more fully the value and importance of what we humans do with our lives and the tremendous difference each one of us can make.

His goal obviously was to help take me out of some of my selfishness and navel gazing to give my ministry, that year at least, a fighting chance. I'm sure he wondered how I could decide whether to remain a priest if I hadn't become involved in the ministry of the parish. His insight with a story I related to him from my own life spoke volumes to me about a lesson I badly needed to learn.

When I was sixteen, I got my driver's license. Both mom and dad had often taken me in the car with them, to teach me how to drive. They both were patient in teaching me how to back up, parallel park and learn the stick shift. Most often they took me to the cow pasture for my lesson. I said they were patient, not stupid!

I learned fairly quickly how to drive the car. Mom and dad were very helpful in offering practical techniques.

They showed their complete confidence in me a few days before my sixteenth birthday when they told me that if I passed the driving tests, I could take the car out

47

on my own on my birthday. I passed the tests and they kept their promise.

That evening after supper as I was backing out of the driveway, I looked back toward the house and, to my astonishment, there stood mom and dad in the living room with the curtains parted, watching my every move!

I'm sure they wondered if I was going to back into the gasoline barrels where we filled up the tractor with diesel fuel. My first thought was, *I guess they don't trust me, after all.*

As I look back now, I realize that I shouldn't have blamed them. After all, I had never learned how to back up a wagon hitched to a tractor! My spiritual advisor drew some important lessons for me in my telling that story, helping him to become better acquainted with me. He told me how he didn't believe that God would stand in the living room with the curtains parted. He said he thought God wouldn't be paying any attention at all to me backing out of the driveway.

"Why not?" I excitedly wanted to know. "Doesn't God watch our every move, always concerned about each one of His creatures?" I asked.

"Well, yes, I'm sure He does. But my point, in light of your selfishness and self pity is that, unlike your parents at that moment, God always totally trusts us. He trusts us so completely, in fact, that it's kind of scary. He really does allow us to be His co-creators, to help Him fashion and form the world by what we say and do.

"When He is preparing to go back to the Father, He tells the disciples, 'Now you go out and teach the nations and baptize them.' He puts things in their hands, and, down through the centuries, into our hands. We are His hands and His feet and if the world is going to know His message, the Good News He came to give us, it's up to us to bring that Good News to others. We certainly know that He is there to inspire us and guide us in that task but He wants us to use our talents, our gifts, our personalities, our spiritualities to bring that message to others, to all whom we meet, to the world.

"Each one of us, as a unique person, is given the task, the responsibility, to put our own special stamp on that message and, by doing so, we show the world a particular part of the face of Christ to others.

"It's amazing to me that God puts such a noble and important responsibility in our hands. He really does totally trust us, just like He did those disciples and so many of His followers down through the ages.

"It's very understandable that your parents watched you from the living room as you backed their car out of the driveway. But I don't think God watches over our shoulders, at least not in a paternalistic or maternalistic way. He doesn't micromanage. He puts us in charge and says you are My co creators. What you say and what you do will, to a great extent, help determine and fashion the kind of world there will be. You are My hands, My feet, My messengers.

" 'If the world is going to know Me,' He seems to be reminding us, 'and know that My message can touch hearts and heal divisions, then it is you, it is you and Me who together can make that happen. And, if you decide not to teach the world about Me and the message I have come to give you, then the world will not know Me.' "

That particular spiritual direction session was key in teaching me the challenge, the task that is set before each Christian, each Catholic, by the very nature of our Baptism as a Disciple of the Lord. I had assumed that responsibility all the more as a Religious and as a priest, a leader of the Christian community.

My spiritual advisor enlightened me as well with some ancient history I had not known: The Greek empire was at the zenith of its power and influence three hundred years before the birth of Christ. During this period of Alexander the Great, the Greeks were winning wars and conquering neighboring lands. The size of their empire, however, created a problem for them. They needed to communicate quickly and effectively from one end of the empire to the other.

Because they were engaged in so many battles in various parts of this vast empire, they needed to be able to quickly send military reinforcements to various strategic points throughout the empire to aid them in battle, to conquer even more territory. To this end, they developed a unique, and effective, system of communication. They dispatched the swiftest runner in each major town and village to race from one place to the next, in relay fashion with other runners, to inform the military whether the battles being waged were successful and some of their soldiers could be dispatched elsewhere or, whether the battles being fought were unsuccessful, land was being lost, and more soldiers were needed in that part of the empire.

If the messenger in a given place was able to bring good news that the Greeks were conquering more lands and the empire was growing, he would be feted as the guest of honor at a festive banquet. If, however, he brought the bad news that the Greeks were losing the battle, land was being lost and soldiers were being killed, the messenger himself was killed.

The Greeks believed there was no distinction between messenger and message; they were one and the same. In fact, the messenger, in their eyes, was even held somehow responsible for the type of news he brought. In the Old Testament the Israelites perceived their God in a somewhat similar fashion. They understood that when God spoke, His proclamation to them was already taking place. There could be no distinction between word and event on the part of God. The event God was proclaiming was already taking place, even as He still spoke.

In modern society we have become all too familiar with the expression, "the check is in the mail." In our modern day experience, there is often a separation, a chasm, between word and event.

Put another way, we Christians don't always live the Good News we sometimes proudly — and loudly — proclaim.

My spiritual advisor helped me see the importance of a oneness in my person between messenger and message. Preaching eloquently on Sunday morning the message of service and forgiveness and compassion and honesty carried a heavy weight with it.

I left his office that day determined to give Oblate life and priesthood my utmost effort. How could I make an honest decision to stay or leave — at least until Christmas — if I didn't give it my all?

Chapter Five:
Forgiveness: A Key to Happiness

With continued help from my spiritual advisor, part of my life began to get better that first year after ordination. I enjoyed meeting the good people of the parish. Many of them took me under their wing, so to speak, and I am fully aware that they are some of the folks who first taught me how to be a Religious and a priest. My family, my friends, the Missionary Oblates, and so many good people who support the works of the Oblates have played, and continue to play, a significant role in that as well.

After I had been in McCook about three months, a man by the name of "Uncle Ted," whom I had met a few weeks previously, asked me if I would join him and his family at their family reunion in the city park that afternoon. I was anxious to meet more of the people of the area and I was dreading another long Sunday afternoon alone in the rectory. I quickly told him "yes."

That Sunday afternoon turned out to be a beautiful late October day. Uncle Ted and I were sitting at a park bench discussing everything under the sun and nothing of any real significance. It was very relaxing.

Suddenly, I noticed that Ted's facial expression changed. His muscles tightened and beads of sweat began to form on his brow. Soon, I realized that he was aware that someone was walking toward our bench. She stopped directly in front of me, looked at me and quickly introduced herself as "Aunt Bertha." She glanced over at Ted but said nothing. Ted was now even more nervous than before. Bertha quickly walked on, barely staying long enough for me to introduce myself.

After she left, Ted said nothing for quite awhile. Only after I began to speak could I get a response from him.

Throughout the rest of the afternoon, I only saw Bertha from a distance. It seemed to me that those who spoke freely with her did not talk to Ted and vice versa. I spent the majority of the afternoon with Ted so I did not have the opportunity to speak with Bertha the remainder of the day.

Late in the afternoon, a photographer stopped by to provide a remembrance of this strange afternoon. He was lining up this sizeable crowd so the best possible picture could be taken. Unbeknownst to him, he positioned Ted and Bertha in close proximity of one another. That decision quickly changed the tenor of the laughter and lightheartedness of the group. Those in the vicinity of Ted and Bertha were now saying very little and others farther away were quietly whispering all the while we were being positioned for the picture.

Shortly after the picture was taken, there seemed to be a mass exodus from the park. Ted said a quick, nervous goodbye to me and I didn't see Bertha as she was leaving. The tension that day had been pointed enough to preoccupy me late into the evening. I awakened several times in the night, wondering what might have happened to cause such distress and anxiety among so many in that family.

I was eating breakfast the next morning when the phone rang. It was Ted.

"Father, I imagine you are wondering what happened yesterday."

"Well, yes, it did cross my mind," I subtly responded, trying my best to disguise my peaked interest.

"It all happened at a family funeral a number of years ago, a fight over an inheritance. I really don't remember a lot of the details. About all I do remember are the people who won't talk to me. Sometimes, I even forget that and start to talk to them. Usually, they just ignore me then. It's sad, huh, Father?"

"Yes, it is, Ted, very sad," was all I could think to say.

"Well, I guess I should let you go. I know you are busy."

With that, Ted hung up the phone. He never spoke to me about it again.

For many days after, I thought about that Sunday afternoon and my phone conversation with Ted. The tremendous tension and anxiety that can be created when two people have refused to forgive each other and the number of lives their bitterness can affect is often a huge burden for all concerned. Their lack of forgiveness and compassion had obviously forced other members of the family to take sides. Most of them are probably not even aware of what happened so long ago at that funeral.

St. Paul is right when he tells us that when one member of the body is hurting, the whole body is in pain. Our actions and our attitudes do have serious consequences and repercussions within and among families as well as for the wider community.

That following weekend I preached to the people of St. Patrick's about compassion and forgiveness. I don't remember the texts of the readings for that Sunday but, at the time, I didn't care what the texts were. The uncomfortableness and nervousness I felt that Sunday afternoon in the city park and how those events preoccupied me for days afterwards, told me a lot about the importance of forgiveness. I was determined to preach on the importance of forgiveness at the weekend Masses, having experienced its value dramatically firsthand.

I really believe a forgiving heart and a compassionate spirit are the practical, down to earth litmus test of whether or not we are living the gospel message of Jesus in our everyday lives.

I had yet to realize in my own life that knowing it and living it are two very distinct realities and challenges.

I was not at St. Patrick's very long when I began to realize that the Pastor, Fr. Cyril Foppe, O.M.I., and I were having some personality clashes. Father Cyril was from the "old school," as they say, and his expectation was that, as pastor, he could call the shots. For the most part, at least in the beginning, I didn't mind. I was usually assigned the 6:30 a.m. Mass for the Religious Sisters who taught in the parish grade school, although I would have preferred to preside and preach more often at the school Mass at 8:30 a.m.

Brother Lon Konold, O.M.I., and I were given the responsibility for visiting the parishioners in the local hospital. It was good ministry for both of us but neither of us looked forward to it. I was so much into my own personal and vocational issues that visiting parishioners who were sick seemed to only occupy time which I felt I could be using in a more productive, if selfish, way.

Brother Lon and I accepted our fate, however. Besides, Fr. Cyril was kept busy with the administrative tasks of running the parish and the school and couldn't be expected to visit the hospital often.

Brother Lon and I taught religion in the grade school and, through our acquaintance with the students in our classes, got to know many of the parents as well.

They were quick to invite us to their homes. They often told us that they couldn't remember having a young priest, let alone a young deacon, at the parish.

We often visited their homes together and, more often than not, the conversation centered on religion and faith. They were lively, interesting discussions and Brother Lon and I sometimes visited with them late into the night.

I was not aware at the time that Fr. Cyril's understanding of "proper behavior for clergy" meant that priests are to be in the rectory no later than 10:30 p.m., and the only exception would be "an emergency sick call."

My only ministry responsibility on Saturday mornings was the Sisters' Mass at 11:00 a.m. That meant that Friday nights were the ideal time to visit parishioners and be able to stay late.

After Brother Lon and I had stayed out well past 10:00 p.m. several Friday nights in a row, I returned home with him to find a note under my bedroom door from Fr. Foppe.

"Father Lou, please take the 7:30 a.m. Mass at the parish tomorrow morning." It was signed, *"Fr. Cyril."*

I was quickly understanding his remedy for the problem. However, at twenty-seven years of age, I could easily burn the candle at both ends. Our late Friday nights continued, the notes under my door continued and I continued taking the 7:30 a.m. Mass. "No problem," Brother Lon and I reasoned.

The two of us were quickly forming a strong alliance against Fr. Cyril. Brother Lon and I had been friends for many years previously but now much of our time together was spent talking negatively about Fr. Cyril.

My sadness and frustration over Uncle Ted and Aunt Bertha's dilemma was forgotten. I hadn't learned anything from that day in the city park, even as uncomfortable and nervous as I had been that Sunday afternoon.

On the first Friday afternoon of Lent, Fr. Cyril

called Brother Lon and me into his office.

"I have a rule that I must enforce with the two of you. All of us will be in this rectory every night at 10:30 p.m. unless there is an emergency sick call. Do you understand?"

He announced this to us in his usual soft-spoken manner, but the message was crystal clear. There were to be no exceptions, save an emergency.

Brother Lon and I never considered not complying with his wishes. We never thought about any alternative action. His demand was clear and we decided we would obey.

Obey we did but show him kindness or compassion we did not.

Throughout the rest of the spring, few words were spoken among all three of us. Brother Lon and I avoided him.

The worst part of the day was the evening meal and the morning and evening prayers. Chance meetings in the rectory hallway were also cumbersome and uncomfortable.

In late spring of that year, I was told that I was being reassigned to St. Henry's High School Seminary in Belleville, Illinois, where I would teach seminarians. Brother Lon would be ordained a priest in June and was being assigned to Norway to help open a new Oblate mission there.

While the tension at the rectory was, at times, quite unbearable, I now knew I wouldn't be there past the middle of May. No need to resolve anything, I told myself. After all, I'll probably never see Fr. Cyril again.

How I could have been so naïve not to realize that, as a fellow Oblate, I would undoubtedly see him at meetings and retreats in the future, now amazes me.

And that's how my time at St. Patrick's in McCook came to a close. I didn't even go upstairs to Fr. Cyril's office at the rectory to tell him goodbye when I left there to go home.

My parents and my sister June and her husband Verne drove from Wesley to McCook to collect me and my belongings in late May. Both my mom and June quickly assessed the situation and saw the tension among all of us.

As we were walking out of the rectory, June asked me if I had said "goodbye" to Fr. Foppe.

"Yes," I said quickly, hoping she would not ask me anything further. She and mom were only trying to help relieve some of the tension they witnessed. I wanted no part of any attempt of a solution.

After spending two relaxing weeks on the farm in Iowa, my brother David drove me to Belleville in the early part of June so I could begin studies toward a Master's degree in Education Administration and Supervision. I would be principal of our high school seminary and needed this degree for compliance with state school certification.

I was ready — even anxious — to pursue any ministry offered to me after such a difficult year in McCook. Besides, those two weeks in Iowa were exactly what the doctor ordered. I discovered that with the grace of ordination came the further grace from my parents of not asking me to do any of the farm chores.

Dad didn't even ask me to hoe thistles out of the corn fields. Wonders never cease, I told myself!

Dad and my brothers, David and Elmer, and my sisters, June, Carolyn, Suzanne and Muriel, relentlessly teased me — I think it was teasing — about what an easy life priests have. They teased about how I had apparently gained some weight in McCook, and about how I would learn to appreciate the beautiful state of Iowa more if I joined them in the corn field to hoe thistles. And so I did. My sister Carolyn even offered me money if I helped clean the house! I helped empty her piggy bank.

I began my studies in mid-June and enjoyed the academic climate of Southern Illinois University at Edwardsville, Illinois. I settled easily into becoming a student again and began preparing for the classes I would be teaching to our high school seminarians that autumn.

As I was getting into my car early one morning in late July to go to school, I noticed someone walking across the seminary campus, quite a distance away. I focused more closely and recognized that unmistakable gait. It was Fr. Cyril! Approximately the same moment that I noticed him, he looked at me. He stared at me for a while; I think to be sure it was me. I stared back for a brief moment and then continued getting into my car. There was no way I was going to walk over to him, much less even talk to him. I asked myself why he would be here, of all places.

I suddenly remembered that he was originally from the Belleville area and was probably staying at the seminary while on vacation visiting family.

Just that quick he yelled my name, and as I sat frozen in the car, he quickened his gait in my direction.

Still sitting there frozen, I wound down the window as he approached the car. He quickly extended his hand to me. Only reluctantly, I did the same.

"Lou," he said confidently, "what happened in McCook is forgotten as far as I'm concerned. I'm sorry for whatever I did that made life there difficult for you. Can we be friends again?"

I couldn't easily or quickly process what had just happened.

Finally, I was able to say, "Cy, I'm sorry, too."

With that, a slight smile came across his face and he said simply, "I'll probably see you later. I'm staying here while I'm on vacation."

With that, he quickly turned and walked into the Oblates' residence.

If there was one person whom I never thought I would — or could — learn much from, it was Fr. Cyril. But it was from him that I learned one of the most valuable lessons of the gospel: compassion and forgiveness.

Father Cyril and I never spoke about our struggles in McCook again. We did often share stories and jokes together as well as the latest news about parishioners we both knew when we would see each other at Oblate meetings or during the summer when he returned to the area for vacation.

Since then, I have become friends with his extended family. Two of his nephews, Tom and John, were in the college seminary when I was Director of the college seminarians in Omaha. I hope I treated them more kindly than I treated Fr. Cyril in McCook!

Father Cyril not only forgave me, he took the initiative to extend the hand of friendship. I have not forgotten the power that such a good example can give.

I remember, as a young boy, attending my oldest sister's wedding. June and Verne were married in April 1955 and mom proudly displayed their wedding pictures on a table in the center of the living room. She kept the pictures there for a long time but finally packed them up and carefully placed them in a box in her and dad's bedroom closet. I knew she was very proud of those pictures and of her first daughter's happy marriage.

A couple months after the pictures had been carefully packed away, I cajoled my younger sister Muriel and younger brother Elmer to "play Mass" with me. It was easy to convince them to do so since Holy Communion consisted of a small round piece of candy! This was a favorite pastime of mine at a young age, a possible premonition of my future calling. Being the oldest of the three, I determined that I could make the rules. Actually, there was only one rule: I was the priest and they were the servers. Being several years younger, they undoubtedly felt there was no alternative for them if they wanted to play. Besides, they did like that candy.

I took the responsibility to get everything ready for Mass: a goblet from the china cabinet for the chalice, round candy pieces for the Hosts, grape juice for the Precious Blood, linen cloths for the purificator and the corporal.

I had noticed at Mass that the priest used an item

about which I had only recently become familiar. It was called a pall. It is a white, cardboard-like square covering for the chalice after the wine has been consecrated. The pall prevents any debris from falling into the Precious Blood.

Mom was always so generous in letting us kids use any of her possessions in the house, even for play. She even allowed me to use her crystal goblet for a chalice.

But where would I find a pall, I asked myself. She had nothing like that in her prized possessions.

Suddenly the answer came to me. The pure white cardboard back of one of my sister's wedding pictures would perfectly fit the bill. I wouldn't be ruining the picture itself, merely the back that made it possible to stand them upright for display, I reasoned. Besides, mom had already displayed those pictures in the living room for several months. There would be no need for her to display those pictures again.

Finding a scissors, I bounded up the steps to mom and dad's bedroom closet and immediately found the pictures tucked carefully away in a box in the far corner.

I'll only need one picture, I thought. The rest of them I will put back carefully in the box. She will never know the difference.

Cutting a perfect square is not as easy as it sounds. I was unsuccessful on the first try, and the second, and the third, and several after that. But keep trying I did and I was still cutting away when I heard someone climbing the stairs. Before I could hide the pictures, mom was standing before me, looking directly at my work.

"Louis, please give me those scissors," she asked in

a no-nonsense manner.

Although my mom and dad were both the epitome of patience, the thought flashed through my mind that she might hurt me with the scissors. Is that why she wanted the scissors? I asked myself.

Then, just as quickly, the thought came to me that she may, just may, want me to stop ruining the few remaining unruined pictures. She continued her stern look for a brief while.

Once I realized she was not going to use the scissors as a form of punishment, I quickly re-focused on my disappointment at not yet having cut a square pall.

I handed the scissors to her.

She must have noticed the sadness in my expression.

And then she knelt down beside me, picked up one of the pictures, and cut out for me a perfectly square pall.

"There you go," she said and smiled faintly.

Chapter Six:
Relationships Renew Us

The seven years I ministered at St. Henry's High School Seminary passed by quickly. The time seemed to fly by primarily because of how busy we all were. The majority of the day was spent teaching. Later in the afternoon, we were often refereeing or coaching sports events for the students, and evenings were consumed with spiritual direction and preparing classes for the next day.

Summers were no vacation, either. Although the students went home for the three summer months, many of the Oblate teachers, including myself, spent that time taking classes and working toward a degree.

The State of Illinois required that a school principal attain a Master's degree in Educational Administration and Supervision which I achieved after three summers. The following four summers — with some classes in the fall and spring semesters — I spent pursuing a doctoral degree at St. Louis University. I received the doctorate in the Philosophy of Education in 1984.

Although I was busy and time passed quickly, I soon realized that teaching, studying and spending time with high school students was not fulfilling me emotionally and spiritually.

Life in community with the other Oblates was very rewarding. We often spent some time together in the evening, talking over events of the day, arguing theology, or playing a board game or cards.

I knew what I missed: families.

Through ministry at neighboring parishes on weekends and by acquainting myself with some of the local families of our seminarians, I began to really feel happy and fulfilled as an Oblate and a priest for the first time.

By this time, some of my good friends who were with me in seminary and in community had already left the priesthood. I kept in contact with many of them and they had told me about their loneliness, their frustration with a pastor, their desire for companionship. I was quickly reminded of my time in McCook. It was my conversations with them that encouraged me to again seek out a spiritual advisor.

Spiritual direction was the catalyst that got me through my difficulties in McCook, and, before that, in my seminary years. I hoped it would keep me spiritually focused in the years ahead.

Once again, my advisor, an Ursuline Sister wise beyond her seventy-plus years and trained in the art of spiritual direction and discernment, gave me good advice.

She spent countless hours with me during those seven years, telling me of the importance of relationships. She spoke more to me about my relationship with God than with others. But she knew about the balance — and the need — for both. She also introduced me to the need for balance in my life in other areas as well. She shared with me about balance in relationships, with both God and others, balance in exercise, eating, praying, playing, drinking, everything. But, again, knowing and doing can be two different things.

Like Fr. Cyril, she was effective in what she said because of how she lived.

My discussions with her those seven years centered almost completely on the topic of relationships. She believed they are the key to a life of completeness, fulfillment, both here and in the hereafter.

Only now, do I understand how wise she was.

I shared with her at our first session my need for adult relationships.

"Teaching high school students is rewarding," I told her, "but I don't have much opportunity to interact with families, with how most people live."

She listened patiently and then launched into a story, the purpose of which was at first lost on me.

"Several years ago, when my dad bought a car, he set up a payment plan with the car dealer. The dealer asked him to sign an agreement whereby my dad promised to make a payment each month toward the total purchasing price of the car. The dealer, who had never met my father before, made it clear to him that if he was negligent with his payments, the car would eventually be repossessed. It's as simple as that. If my dad makes the payments, he can keep the car. If he doesn't, the car will be taken away from him. That is the agreement, the contract that the dealership sets up with him and with all their customers."

She paused and I was speechless.

Where is she going with all this? I wondered to myself.

"But it's not like that with God," she whispered.

And where is she going with that? I still wondered.

"It's not like that with God," she said again.

"God has not established a contract or agreement with you or me or anyone else. He has set up a Covenant with us. Covenant and contract are very different. But it's difficult for us to understand the full meaning of Covenant because the idea of Covenant is so foreign to us. By the term "Covenant" God says to us that He is the one who initiates the relationship with us. He begins the relationship and He is also the one who will never break the relationship, no matter what. So even if we human beings decide to reject Him, abandon Him, deny Him or forget Him, He will always be there for us, ready to take us back, rejoicing that we have come back to Him.

"It's the story of the Prodigal Son; it's the story of Hosea and his unfaithful wife in the Old Testament; it's the story of the woman caught in adultery; it's the story of the woman at the well; it's the story continually repeated in the lives of the people who come to Jesus. Simply put, it's the story of Jesus' life."

Although I had expressed the need for more adult relationships in my life, my spiritual director quickly picked up on the fact that I needed also to progress in my relationship with the Lord. The two must go hand in hand; without the one, the other cannot be truly life-giving and renewing.

We continued with our discussions about the importance of relationships. We spoke about the relationship that is found even in the inner life of God, the Trinity.

Could any human being ever imagine or dream up a God Who is Three, yet One? Could anyone think up God who is Father, Son, and Spirit and each of the Three is a total, complete, perfect Gift to the Other? It is community in its most perfect form. It is relationship totally complete and fulfilled.

My advisor even went so far as to say that if she were asked to define all theology; all of our understanding of God and His creation, she would sum it up in the one word: relationship.

The message of the Old Testament, the message of Covenant, and the message of the New Testament, the Covenant that is perfected and fulfilled in the person of Jesus Christ, is totally about relationship. It is about a God who is madly and passionately in love with His people.

We discussed the simplicity of the message of the Good News of Jesus. Through the centuries, we have complicated it to the point where it has sometimes become unrecognizable.

Many people seem to equate the Good News and faith and religion with rules and regulations. They view the Church as a set of rules and regulations that must be strictly adhered to and on that basis alone will they be judged.

They have lost sight of the fact — if they ever

understood it in the first place — that religion and faith and the Good News is first and foremost about a God who loves His people deeply, about a God who initiates the relationship with us, will always be there for us, will take us back the very instant we decide to come back to Him. That is the primary theme of both the Old and New Testaments.

It is also about a God Who judges, Who holds us accountable, Who expects and asks that we obey Him. That is vitally important for our eternal salvation. But it is first, and foremost: the Good Shepherd story, the Hosea story, the King David story, the woman caught in the act of adultery story, the calling of Matthew story, the Prodigal Son story. Those stories take center stage in God's call to the people of Israel and in His call to Jesus to become man for our salvation.

The relationships I found with some of the parents of our seminarians as well as the people I met in the neighboring parishes of the seminary afforded me the opportunity for weekend ministry.

After Mass, I would make it a point to greet the parishioners as they left church. One morning, I was approached by a young couple who asked me if I would preside at their wedding and also prepare them for marriage. I knew the pastor of this parish rather well and knew that he would not mind if I prepared them for the Sacrament of Marriage and witnessed their marriage vows. I set an appointment with them to begin instructions.

The first meeting between the couple and the priest usually involves filling out the required paperwork for the Church. The paperwork helps ensure the freedom of the couple to marry, i.e., that neither party feels coerced to marry the other, that they are freely giving of themselves to each other.

To help ensure more complete freedom to speak honestly and openly, the priest interviews each of the parties separately. I asked each of them who would like to be interviewed first.

"I'll go first," the groom-to-be excitedly announced.

I quickly got through the series of questions required by the Church. All seemed well.

"I love Susan very much," Dan proudly proclaimed at the end of our interview.

Next, it was Susan's turn. She, too, promptly proclaimed her love for Dan. She answered all the questions as expected and was beginning to get up from the chair when she quickly sat back down again and, with a puzzled look on her face, blurted out, "Father, can I ask you a question?" I thought for sure it would be about flowers or candles or the maximum number of bridesmaids.

"Do you think I should worry about the fact that Dan always shows up at the places where I'm at when I'm out for the evening with my friends or my family or my parents? I'm talking about the nights when I'm not with him but I've told him what I'm doing and where I'll be. Should that be a concern for me?"

"I think you've already answered the question for yourself," I said.

"What do you suppose it means?" she said.

"Shall we call in Dan and see what we can find out?"

"Yes," she quickly answered.

We talked late into the night.

Dan was finally able to admit — though sheepishly — that he did find it difficult to trust Susan completely. He loved her very much, no mistake about that, but when they weren't together, he just wanted to make sure she wasn't with anyone he "needed to worry about." For him, it was not a problem. For Susan, it was.

Susan began to realize that Dan didn't trust her. He couldn't believe her, take her at her word. She saw how damaging this could be to their marriage, to their lifelong relationship. After several more discussions, Susan decided that Dan couldn't love her. It wasn't that he didn't want to; he couldn't. He couldn't trust; he couldn't give her freedom.

I used Dan and Susan's situation to explore with my spiritual advisor God's relationship with me.

At all costs, God gives us freedom. It is scary how much trust and freedom He gives us, as I learned from the time I took my parents' car for the first time. That complete freedom makes it possible for us to choose to accept or reject Him. We can certainly find the consequences of those times we have chosen to reject Him.

The tragic, sometimes horrific events of the 20th century alone are blatant reminders of how our rejection of Him can create unspeakable horrors in our world. Two world wars, concentration camps, nuclear weapons, broken relationships, abuse in all its forms, lack of care for our planet, unspeakable violence, are simply a few of the many horrible consequences caused by mistrust, misunderstanding, desire for power and hatred of each other.

Even with all this tragedy, God still gives us our freedom. He allows us to continue to create this kind of world.

Why?

I think the answer has a lot to do with that couple who came to me for marriage instructions. Dan couldn't allow Susan to be free and so no relationship between the two of them was possible. Only when both parties are able to freely choose one another, trust one another, believe in one another, can there exist a loving, freeing relationship.

God wants to be in relationship with each one of us. It is His desire, His passion, His reason for creating us, His reason for initiating a relationship with us, His reason for always being there to take us back whenever we decide to come back to Him after we have wandered from Him and chosen selfishness and sin.

God won't settle for anything but a completely open, trusting, freeing, loving, relationship. Any kind of relationship other than that is a sham, a slap in the face to God, Who is total love for us.

At any and all costs God wants to love us and for us to freely choose to return that love to Him. Nothing less makes sense to Him.

Dan and Susan never married each other. I stayed in contact with each one of them for some time. Each of them eventually married. Dan has been divorced twice. Susan is happily married with three grown children.

Chapter Seven:
Faith: A Risky Business

During my seminary education, I had set an important goal to be accomplished during the novitiate year. The novitiate year is unlike any other year in seminary formation for men and women preparing for religious life. It is a year of discernment, prayer, learning to live in community, knowledge about one's particular religious community: their ministries, history and the special gifts they bring to the wider Church.

The goal, in my mind, was clear: I would know, for certain, whether or not Oblate life and priesthood was my vocation. And I would know this well before the end of my novitiate year.

At the end of novitiate, the religious life candidate

professes temporary vows. Though these temporary vows would be for only one year, renewable for periods of one year until final vows are professed, I wanted to be certain, before beginning my theological studies, that priesthood and religious life was where God was calling me.

During the first six months of that novitiate year, I was assigned responsibility for the kitchen and dining room. One of the tasks of kitchen duty was setting the tables before each meal.

The day after being assigned this responsibility, I determined that a sure way to discern whether or not God wanted me to become an Oblate of Mary Immaculate and a priest would be to fix in my head a certain number and then, if the number of plates I happened to take from the cupboard matched that number, God was telling me He wanted me to be a religious priest. If the number did not match, He was telling me that religious life and priesthood was not my calling.

There were times when the number of plates matched the number in my mind. And so the answer must be "yes." But there were as many times when the number of plates did not match. I found it difficult to stay with either answer.

Some days, when the number matched, I was excited and enthused. I was feeling attracted to religious life those particular days so I wanted the numbers to match. Other days, when I didn't feel religious life was my calling, I was glad that the number of plates didn't match. Those days, it fit my own plan not to be called by God to religious life and priesthood.

After speaking to my spiritual advisor and novice director, Fr. Tom Hayes, O.M.I., about my struggle with vocational discernment, he helped me understand the foolishness of my thinking. He was a valued blessing for me that entire year.

But more importantly, he helped me understand the process of discernment and how to start the process of discovering God's plan and will for my life.

I finished the novitiate year with a rather clear direction about wanting to become an Oblate priest, but not with as much certainty as I thought the number of matching plates would give me! I left novitiate with a much deeper realization that discernment involves such elements as prayer and relationship with God, spiritual direction, one's own happiness, talents to bring to the particular choice, how one can contribute to the ministries of the religious community.

With that knowledge and the blessing of the Oblate staff at the novitiate, I felt adequately prepared to make my temporary profession as an Oblate of Mary Immaculate.

It has always been tempting for me to try to pin down God, to have Him deal with me on my terms, to find certainty in my relationship with Him.

Lack of clarity in life can be very frustrating. Where is God leading me; what is God saying to me; what is God's plan for me? Why is there doubt? I want to do what He is asking of me, if only He will tell me what He wants of me.

During my years of theology studies, I became

acquainted with many varying theologies of how God reveals Himself and His plan to each one of us. I learned as well that there will never be the kind of certainty I thought I would find in the novitiate with matching the number of plates. God does not deal with us in that kind of fashion. But why not? Why wouldn't God want us to know, with total certainty, what His plan is for us?

Many of the theologians whose works I studied spoke of the reality of a "leap" when trying to understand how God reveals Himself to us. They speak about this leap in terms of our belief in God, in terms of how God reveals Himself to us, in terms of our understanding of who God is in our lives and how He acts in our lives.

Why is there that uncertainty, that leap? Why can't we know for certain what God wants of us, what His will is for us?

That leap serves a vitally important purpose in God's revelation to us, in our understanding how God is present and active in our lives and in the purpose of getting you and me involved in the relationship. God desires a response from each one of us to make the relationship real and true.

When we know something can be proven, such as a mathematical formula, we put the information on a mental shelf after we learn it, to be used whenever needed in the future. We don't continue to ponder the issue of how two plus two equals four, for example. We learn it as a valuable formula, we accept it as true and verifiable from our own experience but we forget about it until we need to recall it as part of our everyday life, in a practical situation, such as in a money exchange. It isn't something we tend to dwell on, however. It doesn't preoccupy us.

What does preoccupy us are precisely those dimensions of our lives about which we can never be certain. They are the most important aspects of our lives: relationships, both with God and with others, trust, faith and love.

It is these aspects of our lives about which we never have complete certainty. I never know for sure, like I do with the mathematical formula of two plus two equals four, that my friend still loves me, that I am called to religious life, that my friend is still being honest with me, that God is faithful to His people. Frustrating as this can be, I believe God made things this way for a very important reason.

It is precisely in the uncertainty, in the leap, that God engages us, that He forces us to break out of our complaisance, mediocrity, apathy to become challenged and committed.

A mathematical formula never requires our commitment, never engages, never challenges. We simply accept it as fact and use it when necessary. God clearly demands more than that from us. Uncertainty, doubt, questioning, provides a challenge for us. It involves us. God won't let us put Him on a shelf like we do with some mathematical formula. He wants us to question, to seek, to probe further, to commit ourselves to Him freely in love and trust. And with a mathematical formula there is never need for us to do that.

From my days of teaching, I am reminded of the

student in class who asks all the questions, showing great interest in the subject matter at hand. He or she wants to know more, to probe more deeply. He or she is involved, interested. That is how God wants His relationship to be with us. We cannot remain complacent; we need to be involved. He wants us to make the leap, the involvement, the challenge. Just like the couple to be married and still <u>not sure</u> of the love, the commitment on the part of the other, they risk with one another in trust, in freedom, and in love.

It is in the leap that we are able to become involved and committed. God wants us involved, committed and challenged. That's when we give of ourselves and God will settle for nothing less. He wants our total being involved. He gave Himself totally to and for us. He asks the same from us.

Faith and our relationship with God cannot be proven, something we can put on a shelf and not think about much. It has to involve every ounce of our being, our fiber. God wants us wholly, entirely, as we should want Him.

Jesus never spoke to me in plates and in numbers. But He did speak to my heart and guided me, ever so gently, without interfering with my desire or my will, toward the Oblates and the priesthood. He has always been there as a consoling, comforting Presence. He has gently led me and guided me. He desires my continued faith and trust in Him even as I remain sometimes uncertain of where He is leading me, of what He is asking of me.

As in any relationship, Jesus asks me, requires me, to give myself to Him in total freedom and trust, to put my life in His hands.

I give myself to You, Lord, in trust and in love. You have led me and guided me and been with me. I continue to rely on Your love and grace. Thank You for Your presence and action in my life.

The strongest desire of the Lord, and the greatest proof of His love for me is that He wants me to share life with Him in His eternal kingdom of justice, truth, love and peace forever. There could be no greater gift desired of God for His people.

Lord, I long to live with You in Your kingdom, where I shall see You face to face forever. Amen.

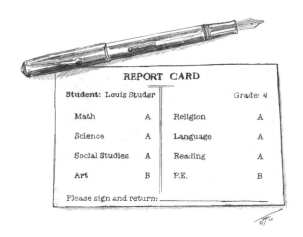

REPORT CARD

Student: Louis Studer   Grade: 4

Math	A	Religion	A
Science	A	Language	A
Social Studies	A	Reading	A
Art	B	P.E.	B

Please sign and return: _____

Chapter Eight:
Prayer: Teach Me About
Your Love for Me, Lord

My parents and family were active members of St. Joseph's Parish in Wesley. Mom belonged to the Catholic Daughters of America and other parish organizations; dad was a member of the Holy Name Society and served as trustee of the parish for many years. My brothers, David and Elmer, and I served Mass and all my sisters and brothers attended St. Joseph's Grade School in Wesley.

The parish school was served by the Sisters of St. Francis of Assisi whose motherhouse was in Milwaukee, Wisconsin. During my grade school years, there were five Sisters in the parish, four of whom taught school and one who served as the cook.

One morning, when I was in the fourth grade, I was kneeling at morning Mass directly in front of my teacher, Sister Mary Vincent. She was someone I greatly admired and liked. She apparently liked our class as well because she was our teacher not only in my fourth grade, but in my fifth and sixth grades as well. It was unusual for the teacher to follow a particular class more than two years. She must have been very convincing to the principal.

As I knelt directly in front of her during Mass, I became preoccupied with the thought that I would be receiving all 'A's' on my next report card. This had been a goal of mine since I had started school four years before but I always received at least one or two 'B's,' usually in the subjects of Art and Science. But during that morning Mass, I became convinced, through a strong, intense feeling that lasted a long time that on my next report card I would receive all 'A's.' While I did not hear any voices, this intense feeling would not go away, much to my delight. Most important of all, I was absolutely convinced that this intense feeling came directly from God. He was answering a prayer I had been offering to Him for over three years.

God does hear my prayers; He does answer my requests, was my recurring thought.

With this feeling still intensely present in my mind and heart even after we walked from the church to the classroom after Mass, I decided to show Sister Vincent the mathematics homework that I had completed the evening before. I remember it was a fairly difficult assignment, multiplying and dividing fractions. I didn't know if I had completed the assignment correctly or not. I showed her my homework which she studied carefully.

After what seemed like a long time, she said, "Louis, you have done everything correctly. I don't believe there is a single mistake. It looks like you will be receiving all 'A's' on your next report card."

I couldn't believe it! God must have spoken to her during Mass as well.

There was no doubt in my mind that God had revealed both to her, and to me, a special sign of His love. He heard, and answered my prayer, not only speaking to me but also to the person who would be His instrument in fulfilling my request, Sister Vincent.

Three weeks later I received my quarterly report card; I received a 'B' in Art. I have no doubt that Sister Vincent forgot what she had said to me and, besides, I'm sure the work I did in Art was not of 'A' quality. What surprised me much more than the 'B' in Art was the fact that I wasn't at all disappointed. I knew God had heard my request and I knew He had spoken to Sister Vincent that morning at Mass. I simply hadn't worked hard enough to attain an 'A' in Art.

God's presence and message to me was not diminished in the least with the 'B' in Art. God powerfully answers prayers, I was certain. That fact doesn't mean that He always meets our expectations or needs but He does hear us and He does answer us, in His own way and in His own time.

I believe that God taught me a very valuable lesson

about prayer at a young age. Our prayers are heard but not always answered in the way we would like.

These moments when I have experienced God's presence and action in my life in a particularly powerful way have been relatively few but tremendously significant. They are those special moments that I often reflect upon in order to conjure up again God's love and presence and action in my life.

I remember as a young boy of about four years of age, my parents took me and my brothers and sisters to the county fair in the nearby town of Algona. Although I don't remember the details very clearly, I do recall that my dad was holding me as we walked through the barns at the fair, seeing the prize cattle, hogs and sheep for which the state of Iowa has become famous.

I think I asked dad if I could walk on my own for a while. He let me down and I ran amongst the pens of the farm animals, especially enjoying the animals that were unfamiliar to me at the time: sheep and ducks and turkeys.

Suddenly, I looked back and didn't see anyone I knew. Where are mom and dad, I wondered. I remember being afraid. All these tall people in this huge building and I didn't recognize a single one of them.

Just that soon, I was swooped up into the arms of a man who was a complete stranger to me. He took me in his arms and I began to cry. He began walking quickly and my fear grew even more intense. And then, suddenly, I saw my mom and dad standing directly in front of me. This strange man had taken me to them.

Mom quickly gave my younger sister, Muriel, to dad and grabbed me from the strange man who had safely delivered me. She profusely thanked the man who had brought me to her and warmly hugged me. She kissed me and was clearly very happy to have me back.

I wish every young child could have an experience similar to that. Although I always knew I was loved by my parents, that kind of experience confirms and affirms that love and care. The story of the Prodigal Son is one I can easily relate to as a result of that experience.

Years later, I asked mom who the man was who found me and brought me to her. She thought for a minute and said, "I don't remember."

I like to think that she was so excited to have me returned to her that she didn't pay much attention to whom it was that brought me back to her. It is the Good Shepherd story and the Prodigal Son story of my life. I wish I could have thanked the man who found me and quickly brought me to mom and dad.

While I was serving as principal and teacher at St. Henry's High School Seminary, I would sometimes visit the Oblate cemetery at the edge of the property. It was a ten-minute walk from our Oblate residence to the cemetery and I often used the occasion to get some brief exercise. Many of the Oblates who had taught me when I was in high school seminary or whom I had ministered with, were buried there.

One snowy, cold December afternoon I attended an afternoon spiritual conference at the Oblate King's House Retreat and Renewal Center, a short distance from the seminary. The topic of the seminar was "The

Kenosis of Christ," i.e., the self-emptying of Jesus.

The speaker focused on how Christ gave of Himself completely for us, how He sacrificed Himself physically, emotionally, psychologically for our sakes, that we might be given the opportunity to one day attain eternal salvation.

I don't remember that the seminar was particularly engaging, but I do distinctly remember the feeling that began to come over me as I drove back to the seminary. I remember as well that I was drawn to walk out to the cemetery.

I parked the car in front of the Oblate residence and began the familiar walk. I walked among the graves and recalled some of the personality traits of the Oblates buried there, especially those whom I had known well.

When I had done this in the past, I would unconsciously recall both the good and bad characteristics of some of the Oblates whom I had known well.

On this particular occasion, I became aware that I was recalling only the positive qualities of each of the Oblates. There emerged inside of me a great gratitude for these men, for their generosity, for their kindness, for their helpfulness to me.

Some of the ones who had taught me in high school seminary were like loving parents for me. They taught me about life; they guided me towards God in the midst of the confusion and anxiety of adolescence. They educated me well and more than adequately prepared me for college academically and spiritually. They continued remarkably the good work that had been started by my mom and dad, brothers and sisters, the good priests and Sisters, as well as the wider community in Wesley, Iowa.

It does take a village and there could not have been a better village than Wesley. The Oblates were able to build on that good beginning.

As I continued to walk among the graves, I was filled with an overwhelming sense of goodness, the goodness of these Oblates and so many other people in my life who had shared, so generously, that goodness with me. Every person I could think of in my life filled me with a feeling of selflessness, love, caring, generosity, including my parents, family, relatives, and friends.

And then my mind and heart focused on the person of Jesus and I thought of the self-emptying love of Jesus that I had heard about earlier that afternoon. As I continued to think about Jesus, I became aware that He was here with me, in this holy place, and that it was He who made possible all the goodness that these people had shown to me and to others in their lives.

I felt very close to Jesus in these moments; I felt I could reach out and touch Him. I was enveloped with a feeling of goodness, love and peace. I recalled some of my own gifts and talents and how Jesus generously bestowed those qualities on me, to be used for others, to build them up, to show them Jesus' love and care for the world.

I stayed in this moment of grace for a long time, though at the end of it, I couldn't believe that almost an hour had passed.

I hadn't been aware that it had gently started

snowing and this made the experience even more beautiful and memorable.

I didn't want to leave the moment but somehow it gradually began fading. The truth of what happened would never leave me; I knew that even as the experience began to subside. I like to think that as the experience faded, it became a deeper part of my being, to be always with me.

When my mother died, a little more than ten years ago, I knew immediately what I would say at her funeral homily.

In my mom's later years, as she became more frail, I began to appreciate more and more the many delicious, large meals she had prepared throughout her lifetime. Mom lived on a farm as she was growing up and she helped cook for farmers who would gather to harvest the crops and, after she married, she continued to do the same. There were often eight to ten adults at each of these meals, not including the children present.

These hardworking farmers were big eaters and they expected a full meal, even at noon: fried chicken, potatoes, bread, butter, corn on the cob and pie with ice cream for dessert was typical bill of fare.

Mom would kill the chickens that morning, dress them and fry them, dig potatoes from the garden and bake the pies, even making the crust. Breakfast would consist of fried eggs, bacon, toast, butter, coffee and juice. Besides that, she would often bring afternoon lunch to the farmers working in the fields. Lunch was sandwiches, cookies and juice. This was the fourth meal of the day, added on to a full breakfast, complete dinner at noon and hearty supper as the sun went down.

I remember fondly that mom, on many days, had blood splashed on her legs in the summertime from the chickens she had killed herself that morning. My sisters, June, Carolyn, Suzanne and Muriel had learned that art as well, including gutting, dressing and cleaning, then frying the chickens. They were quick learners because they had an excellent teacher.

No one could have taught the values of love and service better or more effectively than mom did by her own quiet example. Her example of service was infectious.

The gospels are filled with the importance of service, spending our lives in love for others. The life of Jesus is our best example. He truly is the complete self-emptying, compassionate love of the Father for us. He spends His life with the poor, the lepers, the blind, the lame and gives totally of Himself on the Cross that we might have life with Him forever.

In my prayer, I often think about mom and dad's selfless love and service for me and for my brothers and sisters and even for the wider community. Their example leads me to strive to follow Jesus more closely through a life of service for others.

Prayer is the ingredient that gives me the strength, the desire, to follow Jesus in giving myself to others. Remembering the generous service of people in my life leads me to want to pray.

For many years in my life, prayer was an activity

that I dreaded and felt guilty about. For the most part, I didn't enjoy it nor did I feel that I benefited much from it. I recognized the value of praising and thanking God as a worthwhile endeavor but my prayer often consisted in asking a favor, praying for someone who had requested me to do so or in saying rote prayers such as novena prayers or the rosary.

As with so many of the important issues in my life, my spiritual advisor helped me realize that my understanding of prayer can make a big difference in my approach to prayer.

Prayer and relationship go hand in hand.

What is prayer? My spiritual advisors and parents, over the years, have taught me a lot about prayer.

First and foremost, I view prayer as relationship. Prayer is the way I can become more aware of how much God loves me and, therefore, how I can respond to that love.

Prayer is also an awareness that God always takes the initiative in the relationship and that He will never withdraw that love from me. His love for me is unconditional: no matter how much I choose to distance myself from Him, God will never distance Himself from me. He will always be there for me, ready to take me back in total love and forgiveness. Like the poster I once saw, aptly stated, "If I feel distant from God, guess who's moved?"

As Perfect Love, God cannot draw away from me. The Covenant idea in Scripture says it clearly: God begins the relationship and He continues to try to bring me back to Him when I have withdrawn from Him

94

through sin and selfishness. God can do nothing other than what is total, complete, perfect love and self-giving to His people.

My brothers and sisters and I learned the value of prayer early in our lives. Mom and dad knelt together in prayer every morning before we went to school. They were insistent that we pray the rosary and even a few other prayers as well, almost every evening. They knew that prayer was key in growing in their own relationship, and in their knowledge and love of the Lord. They wanted their children to learn this value as well.

Prayer, then, is recalling, remembering and re-intensifying God's presence and action in our lives. It is rediscovering those moments that we have experienced God intensely. It is rediscovering that God intensely loves us and it is generously choosing to respond to that love and to the compassion and forgiveness that is always there for us, whenever we are ready to receive it once again.

Prayer is finding God in the generosity and service of others. It is God who initiates, who makes possible that generous service. It is God's Spirit Who prompts us to prayer, Who moves our hearts to want to praise and thank God. There is nothing good that happens in our world or in our own lives that is not initiated by the power and action of the Spirit.

Prayer is praising God for His goodness. It is thanking Him for His generosity. It is recognizing that all we have is gift from Him.

Sometimes, prayer reminds me of a married

couple, married for fifty or even sixty years, who sit on their front porch swinging together evening after evening, saying little to one another. It is enough for each of them merely to be in the presence of the other. They know everything about each other. They know deeply of their love for each other. Little needs to be said between them anymore. It is sufficient for them to sit together, to swing together, to be with each other.

Sometimes, we can get the notion that prayer is trying to change God, to alter His plans to match ours. Prayer is not that. It is allowing ourselves to grow in our awareness of how much God has loved us, how He has been active in our lives, how, where and when He has been revealing Himself to us.

Prayer is also responding to that initiative, that love, that compassion and forgiveness. It is discovering God more deeply in moments of quiet and reflection, in His Sacred Word, in the person of Jesus, in the people whose lives have interacted with our own with their generous, loving example. It is discovering God's Spirit in the gentle breeze, the quiet whisper, the message of the dream.

St. Augustine, Bishop of Hippo, in Africa, knew this gentle presence of the Lord Jesus in his own life. "Our hearts are restless," he said so eloquently, "until they rest in You."

God's deepest, most ardent desire for each one of us as His chosen ones is that one day, after the journey of this life, we would be with Him in the kingdom of truth, justice, love and peace that He has prepared for us from all eternity. He wants us to be with Him in that kingdom forever.

He wants only the best for us, His beloved creatures, the pinnacle of His creation.

My family made sure to get front row at the Mass of Ordination.

I was ordained Deacon at St. Henry's High School Seminary in Belleville, Illinois.

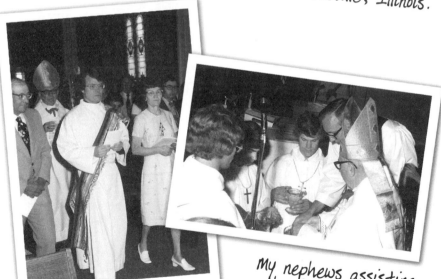

Processing in for the Ordination Mass with my parents and Bishop Greteman.

My nephews assisting the Bishop at the Ordination Mass.

Wishing my dad the sign of peace at the Ordination Mass.

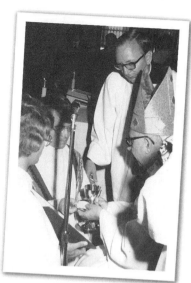

My nephews served the Mass.

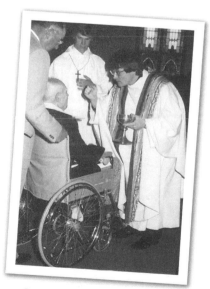

Offering Communion to my grandpa at the Ordination Mass.

It was a great privilege to bless my parents immediately after the Ordination.

A blessing for everyone
at the Mass of
Thanksgiving.

With my parents, Paul
and Marcella, after
the Ordination.

With my parents and brothers and
sisters on Ordination day.

Bishop Frank Greteman
of the Sioux City,
Iowa diocese ordained
me to the priesthood.

Offering my
First Mass!

Above: With the faculty and
staff at St. Henry's High School
Seminary in Belleville, Illinois.

Right: Shortly after Ordination.
I'm ready to begin ministry
at St. Patrick's Parish in
McCook, Nebraska.

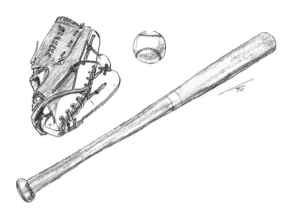

Chapter Nine:
A Meaningful Life

I enjoy buying new shoes. From the time I picked out a red pair in the catalog before entering first grade (maybe I had plans to become pope one day), I have always enjoyed purchasing new shoes.

Every summer, a couple weeks before school started in the fall, my family went shopping for school clothes in Mason City. There was a certain ritual involved with this. We went shopping on August 15th, the Feast of the Assumption of the Blessed Virgin Mary, a holy day of obligation and one of the few weekdays dad didn't work in the summer.

I'm sure that mom and dad expected each year that one shopping trip should be sufficient to purchase everything we needed for another school year. Usually, that would have been the case, except for the fact that until I found the exact color and style of shoe I wanted,

I refused to let mom make a purchase of shoes. And that meant going back to the store until I found exactly what I wanted.

I can only begin to imagine how frustrating this was for her. Usually, I wasn't so picky, so finicky about my clothes. But with shoes, I was.

Reflecting about my exactness in choosing just the right color and style of shoes, however, has led me to consider, even ponder, one of the qualities or attributes of God. I think that God possesses that same unique quality of exact choice when it comes to His creation.

God could never settle for second best. God is choosy, finicky in fashioning us as His creatures. It seems to me that God had a unique, specific plan in mind for creating this beautiful world we live in, and even more so, the creatures He fashioned, most especially us human beings.

In the thirty-plus years since my ordination to priesthood, I have been surprised by the number of people who tell me they are struggling to find meaning in their lives, to discover purpose in their existence. It is as though they can no longer find God. They wonder why they cannot find any signs or messages of God in their lives. They seem not to have lost belief in God but they claim that they no longer experience Him, at any level, in their hearts and in their lives.

This phenomenon is always rather amazing to me. Many of them truly agonize over this seeming meaning-lessness of life. They believe God has abandoned them, but at the same time they seem to know the foolishness of such a belief. A God of love and compassion could never abandon the creatures He made, especially when we consider that He formed and fashioned us with such precision and care. Second best could never do for God.

Probably as a result of lack of prayer in their lives over a considerable period of time, perhaps no longer receiving the Sacraments on a regular basis, or perhaps too little time spent in quiet reflection, they can no longer find God in their lives.

And yet, even with this kind of apathy over a long period of time, I like to remind them about what God has done for them. God's presence and action in every human being's life is abundantly clear. Often, we are looking in the wrong places.

A biologist would be able to tell us that the unique way in which our genes and chromosomes fashioned us physiologically makes you — and me — special and different from any other human being ever created and different from anyone that ever will be created.

A psychologist would be able to tell us that the unique way in which our personality traits and characteristics fashioned our personality makes you — and me — special and different from any other human being ever created and different from anyone that ever will be created.

A theologian would be able to tell us that the unique way in which we view who God is and how He acts in our lives makes you — and me — special and different from any other human being ever created and different from anyone that ever will be created.

God does put a special mark, a unique stamp on each one of us.

Friends of mine, Tom and JoAnn Foppe, are the

parents of identical twins. To me the twins look exactly alike and have since birth. Their personalities seem to closely resemble each other's to the point where I cannot tell them apart in that way either. But their parents tell me they are really very different from one another.

Tom and JoAnn often tell me about the twin's physiological and psychological differences. The individual uniqueness of each child is clear to them, and has been since their births. God loves each one of them, and each one of us, in a special, unique way. He intimately knows each one of us; He calls <u>each one</u> of us by <u>our</u> name, despite the fact that I can never tell the two of them apart.

I was giving a presentation to college students a number of years ago when I was teaching at Creighton University in Omaha. The locus of my talk was a large auditorium and it was packed. I focused my talk on St. Paul's notion that, in and through our baptism in Christ, we become adopted sons and daughters of God, our loving Father.

Although, I thought I had prepared well for the presentation, I could tell the students were not listening very carefully to what I was saying. Many of them were talking to one another, some were sleeping, a few were doing their homework, some were playing with pocket computers. In the midst of all this activity, I noticed there was one young man who seemed to be listening intently to my every word. He clearly stood out as he directly focused his attention on me. I don't think he took his eyes off me throughout the entire presentation.

At the end of my talk, I invited questions. There being none, I began gathering up my notes when I noticed the young man approaching the podium where I stood. He blurted out, "Father, I really enjoyed your talk."

"Thanks," I muttered, "but I think you might be the only one who would say that."

"I think I enjoyed your talk because I'm adopted. My parents told me about it when I was seven years old. They explained to me that more than anything else, they wanted a child. When they were told they could not have a child of their own, they looked into adopting. They told me about the difficulties of adopting a child.

"I know they had to make a couple trips to Eastern Europe, fill out reams of paperwork, spend a lot of money and be carefully checked out to make sure they were the kind of parents who could successfully adopt. It was a long, involved process, they told me. They had to be sure beforehand that this was something they really wanted to do.

"They told me they wanted a boy, from Eastern Europe, so they said they really got to choose. And the choice was all the more exciting and wonderful because of all the time and energy they expended in helping to make the adoption happen. The worst part, they said, was the waiting. It took over two years from the time they began the process, to the time I was in their, our, home."

A big smile came across his face as he said that last sentence. He felt chosen, blessed, loved. His parents certainly seemed special, from the way he described them.

That young man knew what it meant to be picked out as special, as chosen, an adopted son of God.

During my first few years of grade school, recess was a dreaded time for me. Academics were always relatively easy for me but I hated recess. Throughout the fall and spring and even sometimes in the winter, if there was not snow on the ground, we would play baseball.

Previous to beginning the game each day, we would divide into two teams. The two best players in the class were automatically always the captains. This was never questioned. I suppose one team would have been favored over the other if the two best players were on the same team. Every day, the same two guys were the captains. This never changed during five years of playing baseball in grade school.

And then the part of recess I most dreaded would begin. After a coin toss to determine which captain got to choose first, each captain would begin to call out the names of the players he wanted on his team. Of course, the better players would be chosen first and names continued to be called until only one or two players were left standing in the middle, waiting to be called.

Having to stand in the middle, not yet able to go to either side where the teams were, was the worst part. Watching everyone stare and hoping, of course, that my name would not be the last one chosen was an awfully humiliating experience. And, with the last couple players to be chosen, the captain sometimes wouldn't even say the name. More likely, he didn't really care if you played on his team or not but you had to play on one or the other team. So, he sometimes just motioned for you, not even saying your name, to indicate that you were on his team.

My cousin Richard was always one of the captains. Being the best baseball player in the class, he got the privilege every day we played baseball of calling out the names of whom he wanted on his team.

Richard and I were good friends. On days when we didn't play any organized sport, he and I would walk around the playground together, talking about school, our teachers, farm work and how great it was to live on a farm in Iowa. (I think he expressed that sentiment a lot more than I did but I'm sure I agreed with him to avoid an argument.)

On those days that Richard chose our classmates to be on his team, he always made sure I was never chosen last or even second last.

He never chose me first, after all, he did want to win the game! But, towards the end of the choosing, he would call out my name while there was still some dignity left with those of us still standing in the middle.

"Louis," was all he would say but that was more than enough. How good it felt to hear my name! I was chosen. Another day had passed when I wouldn't be left standing there alone, the last one picked.

I know that some other classmates often wondered why Richard chose me in the process before some other classmates who were better players than me. Whether or not they ever said anything to him, I never found out and I never asked.

Richard saved me from what would have been a very humiliating experience many of my grade school days.

I'll never forget his compassion and friendship and how good it felt to hear my name called.

God knows each one of us better than we know ourselves. He calls each one of us by name and chooses us to be His own.

Chapter Ten:
God's Self-Emptying Compassion:
Jesus Christ

The center and focus of the Christian faith is a
person: Jesus Christ. Intellectually, I knew
and understood that. It is one thing to
know this; it is quite another to accept it in one's heart.

The question of Jesus to Peter, "Who do you say that
I am?" had haunted me from my college seminary days.

What was my response to that question? What
meaning and purpose does Jesus have in my life, in
my actions?

About three months before the twenty-fifth
anniversary of my first profession of vows as an Oblate, I
received a phone call from my Provincial, Fr. David
Kalert, O.M.I.

"Would you preach and preside at the Mass celebrating

anniversaries of vows and ordinations this year?" he asked.

"Oh, David," I begged, "there are many wiser and more experienced Oblates celebrating their anniversary year. They would do a much better job."

"No," he said emphatically, as was customary for him, "I would like you to do this."

"Yes, of course," I humbly responded, as was customary for me!

Father David is a friend so that made it difficult to plead further.

"You can use the Scriptures of the day if you wish," he said.

Although the celebration was still three months away, I looked up the readings for the day on which the celebration would take place.

I found a gospel passage with which I was relatively unfamiliar and uneasy. I had never preached on this passage before and when I had come across it in my own reading, tended to avoid it.

I dreaded the thought of writing a homily based on this gospel text and having to preach in front of my peers. Most of the Oblates present would be older and wiser than me and many of them more familiar with the Scripture texts than was I.

I didn't realize then that delving into this text would tell me so much about the person of Jesus.

That text helped answer in a profound way who this Jesus is for me. It gave me a particular insight into how Jesus saw Himself and the mission that had been given to Him by His Father. It has continued to be fruitful prayer for me and help me understand Jesus as friend and companion for life's journey. This was key for me if I was to continue in my vocation as an Oblate priest.

> *From there He set out and went away*
> *to the region of Tyre. He entered a house*
> *and did not want anyone to know He was there.*
> *Yet He could not escape notice, but a woman*
> *whose little daughter had an unclean spirit*
> *immediately heard about Him, and she came*
> *and bowed down at His feet. Now the woman*
> *was a Gentile, of Syrophoenician origin. She*
> *begged Him to cast the demon out of her*
> *daughter. He said to her, "Let the children be*
> *fed first, for it is not fair to take the children's*
> *food and throw it to the dogs." But she*
> *answered Him, "Sir, even the dogs under the*
> *table eat the children's crumbs." Then He*
> *said to her, "For saying that, you may go —*
> *the demon has left your daughter." So she*
> *went home, found the child lying on the bed,*
> *and the demon gone.*

(Mark 7:24-30; New Revised Standard Version. Nashville: Thomas Nelson Publishers, 1989.)

That Scripture passage, from St. Mark's Gospel, is also found in St. Matthew's Gospel, (15:21-28).

Many Biblical scholars believe this dialog between the Syrophoenician woman and Jesus represents a dramatic change in Jesus' own understanding of His mission.

It seems that Jesus understood His mission of

sharing the Good News with God's chosen people, the Israelites. As the chosen people, they are referred to in the Scripture passage as the children (of God), seated around the table.

The Syrophoenician woman, a Gentile, asks Jesus to consider sharing His message, His power of healing, with the Gentiles (non-Jews), i.e., the dogs under the table.

When Jesus sees the faith of this woman and her desire to share in His Good News and healing powers, He recognizes the importance of sharing God's message with the Gentiles as well. His mission is to all people. She suggests that the dogs, too, are hungry and need nourishment.

This passage held great significance for me for a number of reasons: Jesus, in His humanity, is able to recognize, and accept, her wider view of bringing the Good News to the whole world, not merely the people of Israel; the deep faith of this woman is clearly what influences Jesus to accept her suggestion; Jesus, in humility and openness to her, listens to this woman and takes compassion upon her and her daughter's illness. He recognizes that her specific need far outweighs whether or not the first priority, or the only priority, of His mission should be to the people of Israel.

Jesus listens to the people who come to Him in their need in the myriad of situations throughout the gospel. He hears them, understands them and is willing to learn from them as well.

This is truly a God of mercy and compassion and a God in love with His people.

My second favorite passage of Scripture is also quite

revealing about who this Jesus is. Although St. Paul probably did not personally know Jesus, his understanding of Jesus and how Jesus saw Himself is consistent with the passage of Jesus with the Syrophoenician woman. Jesus sees Himself as the humble, obedient servant, open to what His Father asks of Him.

In Philippians 2:5-11, St. Paul writes:

> *Let the same mind be in you that was in Christ Jesus, who, though He was in the form of God, did not regard equality with God as something to be exploited, but emptied Himself, taking the form of a slave, being born in human likeness. And being found in human form, He humbled Himself and became obedient to the point of death — even death on a cross.*
>
> *Therefore God also highly exalted Him and gave Him the name that is above every name, so that at the name of Jesus every knee should bend, in heaven and on earth and under the earth, and every tongue should confess that Jesus Christ is Lord, to the glory of God the Father.*

(New Revised Standard Version. Nashville: Thomas Nelson Publishers, 1989.)

St. Paul is very insightful about who this Jesus is. Jesus gave totally of Himself to and for us, never counting any cost to Himself. He is the compassion and love of the Father for all mankind. This is the total self-emptying of Jesus to do His Father's will.

In the four Gospels, we find Jesus in a myriad of circumstances in which people come to Him with all kinds of needs and requests. It is the man born blind, the woman who is hemorrhaging, those many possessed by demons, the lame, the lepers, the sinners, the woman caught in adultery, the woman at the well and the list goes on and on.

Significant for me in these varied encounters is the response of Jesus to their requests. He treats each person uniquely and differently. He respects where they are at in their lives and responds individually to their specific needs. How consoling that is, to know He deals the same way with each one of us. He has no set formula, no certain pattern of response. He meets us too, where we're at, and leads us forward.

These two Scripture passages became significant for me because they provide keen insight into who this Jesus was and is. Praying over these passages, and others, allowed Jesus to become a caring, compassionate model of ministry for me.

For those who have faith, He grants their request, as He does with the Syrophoenician woman who asks that He heal her daughter. For the woman caught in the act of adultery who suffers extreme humiliation at the hands of her captors, He offers immediate forgiveness and tremendous compassion. For the buyers and sellers in the temple He becomes angry and confronts the arrogance of their actions. For some who seem to lack sufficient faith in Him and His ability to cure, He calls forth an act of faith from them. For those chosen for leadership who lord it over others, He harshly confronts and demands to know whether or not they are willing to serve, rather than be served.

In all these times and places, and in many others besides, He does what is best for the person to lead them along the path of truth and faith and trust in the Father's love for them.

Showing us the Father, pointing the way to eternal life, modeling compassion and truth for us is the mission of Jesus. He empties Himself; He gives Himself totally; He turns His life completely over to the Father because of His intense love for each one of us.

He does not count the cost to Himself; He empties Himself, taking the form of a slave for us. Jesus is the model of how we are to give of ourselves to others in love and service.

Furthermore, this Jesus, Son of God and Son of Mankind, lived on this earth and suffered physically, emotionally, psychologically, not knowing the final outcome.

We know of His fear and anxiety in His Agony in the Garden the night before His death. He pleads with His Father, "If it is possible, let this cup pass by me, yet not My will but Your will be done."

Some medical personnel and psychotherapists maintain that it is possible to sweat blood when one is under extreme duress and anxiety. The Evangelists' recording of Jesus sweating drops of blood on this dark night of His soul may not be mere symbolic expression or illusion but observable fact.

The question must be asked: Did Jesus know, as He suffered in the garden, that all this would end in a glorious Resurrection?

The Church takes no official position regarding the consciousness of Jesus, i.e., the degree to which Jesus was aware that He was the Son of God previous to His Resurrection.

From His cry to the Father in the garden, it seems likely that He did not know the next day's cruel crucifixion would ultimately end in glorious Resurrection. Lacking that knowledge would have made His horrible suffering seem even more cruel and, perhaps, pointless.

In any case, Jesus remains completely faithful to the mission given to Him by His Father in heaven.

Jesus realizes, as He begins His public ministry but perhaps even before that as well, how deeply He must rely on the Father's help to enable Him to endure this life of hardship and resignation.

Undoubtedly, He could see what was happening as He engaged in His public ministry. The crowds were attracted to Him and His teaching because, unlike the religious and political authorities of the day, Jesus lived what He proclaimed. He was true to His word.

The crowds who gathered around Jesus found this most attractive. Finally, they found someone who did not burden them with rules and regulations which these religious and political rulers themselves did not follow. Here was someone who taught forgiveness, compassion, truth and He lived out that message by serving others, putting others' needs before His own, spending His life with sinners, the outcast, the lepers, the blind, the lame and those whom society considered worthless.

Jesus surely was able to see and understand what might finally happen. The large crowds who were attracted to Him would soon become a threat to the religious and political authorities. They had to make their authority felt. They could not give up their power and prestige to this itinerant preacher.

They determined that Jesus had to die.

As some theologians have so aptly expressed, describing the kind of life Jesus lived in our midst: He came so close to us, so intimately a part of us, He even allowed us to kill Him.

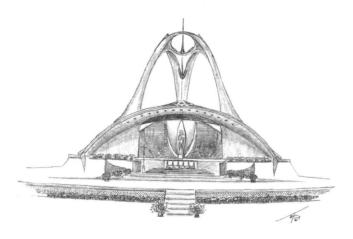

Chapter Eleven:
Heaven on Earth: The National
Shrine of Our Lady of the Snows

Two Oblates whom I had always looked up to and admired were Fr. Edwin Guild and Fr. Floyd Boeckman. Father Guild was the Founder of the National Shrine of Our Lady of the Snows and Fr. Boeckman was his right-hand man while the Shrine was being built and for many years after.

If Fr. Guild had the vision to foresee the importance of a shrine to promote devotion to Our Lady of the Snows, then it was Fr. Boeckman who possessed the practical know-how to make Fr. Guild's vision a reality.

When I was appointed Director of the Shrine in July, 1997, I was well aware that I was standing in the footsteps of two Oblates who were held in high regard by both Oblates and lay people alike. The challenge seemed daunting and even a bit frightening.

For many of the 1.1 million pilgrims who visit the Shrine annually, the Shrine is an idyllic setting to get away from it all and re-discover God's presence in one's life.

Located on 200 sprawling, beautifully landscaped acres, it provides the perfect setting to quietly pray, reflect, read and walk.

Many of our visitors spend at least a couple days at the Shrine, enjoying our first class hotel, restaurant and gift shop amenities, all the while walking the grounds and praying at our many devotional sites. Children of all ages can enjoy our spacious new playground while their parents attend one of the sixty programs and events offered each year.

The Shrine is not always an idyllic place for the 220 employees who make it their livelihood. For them, it is a workplace, but they recognize — and appreciate — the unique atmosphere in which they find themselves. The same is true about the employees at the Missionary Association where supporters of the Oblates request a rosary, ask a question about the ministry of the Oblates or call in for much needed prayers.

I am always delighted to hear stories from our visitors how one or the other employee went the extra mile to accommodate the special need or request of a pilgrim. It happens almost daily.

For me, the role of Director of the Shrine and the Missionary Association has meant straddling the roles of priest and employer, not always an easy combination, but a ministry I have greatly enjoyed. I have learned much more about the business world than I could have ever imagined.

At both places, I have met and spoken with people from all over the world. Their stories are incredible testimonials of a God Whom they love deeply and Who works daily miracles in their lives. Unknowingly, they have strengthened my vocation and my relationship with God. In many ways, living and ministering at the Shrine and the Missionary Association is particularly unique.

The history of how the Shrine was started and the origin of devotion to Our Lady of the Snows is a special and unique story in itself.

Devotion to Mary, the mother of Jesus, under the title of Our Lady of the Snows is one of the oldest devotions to Mary in the Catholic Church. It can be traced to Rome, Italy, in the year 352 A.D. The Blessed Mother had indicated in a dream to a wealthy couple that she wanted a church built in her honor and the site for the church would be covered with snow. The wealthy couple went to see the Holy Father, Pope Liberius, to tell him about their dream. They discovered, much to their surprise, that the Pope had had the same dream.

On the morning of August 5, 352 A.D., all of Rome awoke to a hot, sunny day, yet snowfall covered the top of Esquiline Hill. A church was soon built on this site. The Basilica of St. Mary Major, one of the four major basilicas in Rome, serves as the seat of devotion to Our Lady of the Snows to this very day and is located on this site.

Devotion to Our Lady of the Snows was first introduced to Belleville, Illinois, by the Missionary Oblates of Mary Immaculate. Father Paul Schulte, O.M.I., known as "the flying priest of the Arctic," was a pilot who brought medical aid and supplies to the remote Oblate missions, particularly those north of the Arctic Circle.

To promote devotion to the Blessed Mother among the Eskimo (Inuit) peoples, Fr. Schulte introduced them to the devotion of Our Lady of the Snows.

He commissioned an artist, J. Watson Davis, to paint a picture of Our Lady of the Snows. Davis depicted Fr. Schulte and his airplane on a sick call to an Inuit mission with Our Lady appearing above the mission as in an apparition surrounded by the rays of the Northern Lights. When Fr. Schulte moved to St. Henry's Oblate Seminary in Belleville, he brought this painting with him and it was hung in the chapel.

In 1943, Fr. Schulte and another Oblate priest, Fr. Edwin Guild, O.M.I., together with other Missionary Oblates of Mary Immaculate began a perpetual novena to Our Lady of the Snows at the seminary (July 28th to August 5th, the Feast of Our Lady of the Snows). Soon, the novena became an annual event, attracting thousands of people each year. As devotion to Our Lady of the Snows grew, the grounds at St. Henry's Seminary were not adequate to handle the crowds.

In February 1958, farmland on the bluffs overlooking the Mississippi River was purchased and construction began on the National Shrine of Our Lady of the Snows, one of the largest outdoor shrines in the world.

The Shrine began with the vision of a few Oblates who knew the missionaries in Canada needed prayers to sustain them in their challenging work.

Pope Pius XI called the Oblates "specialists in difficult missions" largely because of the difficulties the Oblates encountered in their work in Canada and the Arctic and in other difficult missions around the world.

The Shrine is much more than a place of pious devotion; it is vibrant, holy ground where 1.1 million visitors each year honor our Blessed Mother — and pray for the missionary works of the Oblates in over 70 countries of the world.

When I assumed responsibility as Director of the Shrine of Our Lady of the Snows and the Missionary Association of Mary Immaculate, I began to ask the employees, "What is the spirituality of the employees at the Missionary Association and the Shrine? Should there be such a spirituality? Should we offer retreat days to our employees? What would be the central theme of such days of reflection and retreat?"

I knew I had asked some worthwhile questions and I decided, with the help of some of the employees, to try to resolve them. We found some answers when we further asked, "Who is our public? Who supports our missionary work and who comes to the Shrine and what are they looking for from us when they visit?"

We began to discover that a spirituality for our employees was important but also a spirituality we could offer to those who visit the Shrine, who write to us, who want to participate more intensely in the charism and missionary work of the Oblates of Mary Immaculate.

We realized that many people who visit us, who write to us, are people who were hurting, seeking healing and needing hope in their own lives and in the lives of others for whom they have been asked to offer prayers. They were asking us to help alleviate their hurts, their struggles and offer them a reason to go on, to continue the journey of life.

A married couple from Pennsylvania whom I met after Mass one winter afternoon captured for me what we were struggling with as a committee.

The woman was recently told she needed kidney dialysis. She and her husband came to the Shrine, expecting that while they were here she would receive a call from a relative offering to donate a kidney. They were here three days and I met them the afternoon before they were returning home. No one had called. Yet she had a bright smile on her face and so did her husband.

"So what happened to give you such a bright smile?" I asked after she told me her story.

"Aren't you afraid of the dialysis?"

"Father, I don't exactly know what happened. I'm still scared but I'm going home tomorrow with an entirely new attitude. My prayers were answered here. I'm not sure what happened. But as my husband and I prayed, I was given the strength to face the dialysis. I know I'll be okay."

Her husband was shaking his head as if to say, "Yes, that's what happened. I saw it with my own eyes."

I told them they should tell others about their experience here. Maybe others who need healing will come here and receive the hope they need to go on, as well.

And thus was born the theme, "Share the Healing and the Hope."

It is our spirituality, our theme, our motto at the National Shrine of Our Lady of the Snows and the Missionary Association of Mary Immaculate.

St. Etienne Elderly Care Center in Haiti is home for this blind man.

Fr. Marc Boivert, O.M.I. at Hope House, a housing program for about 160 young Haitians.

These young Haitians are not very impressed with my attempt at entertaining them.

I'm practicing my awkward French with some young Haitians.

Learning Portuguese from one of Brazil's natives.

With fr. Ed figueroa, O.M.I., and some of his family in Brazil.

Above: I find a bargain at a local roadside stand in Brazil.

Right: I don't think these young Brazilians understood my Portuguese very well.

Left: "He ain't heavy...he's my brother...," might be the comment of this young girl carrying her brother in Madagascar.

Below: These women were preparing a stew for dinner in Madagascar.

There is a joy and love of life among young people everywhere, even in the midst of the poverty of Madagascar.

The Oblates minister to youth in Sri Lanka. Recently the Oblates built an orphanage for young people affected by the tsunami.

Above: Fr. Jeevandra Paul, O.M.I., speaks with some native Sri Lankans who received shelter from the Oblates.

These Sri Lankans are very grateful for all the Oblates had done to help during the civil war there.

Chapter Twelve:
Beyond Iowa: The Oblate Cross Covers the World

As summer after summer passed with hoeing thistles in the corn and bean fields, I continued to wonder if there was any hope for me to ever see a different area of the country, even a different part of Iowa!

When Fr. John Frischmon, O.M.I., visited the seventh and eighth grades and spoke about the Oblates ministering on six continents, I was intrigued. I had no idea that any missionary order was in so many areas of the world. Thousands of Oblate priests and Brothers in such places as Canada, Sweden, Brazil, Congo, Australia, Japan, to name only a few.

It all sounded so exciting that I could hardly believe it was true.

Father John mentioned to us youngsters, both times he visited the school, that Pope Pius XI called the Oblates "specialists in difficult missions." Not only were the Oblates ministering in all four corners of the globe, they were competent and skilled in the work they were doing.

Many years later, in February 2004, I was privileged to meet another Pope, John Paul II. I wanted to tell him about the Shrine of Our Lady of the Snows and, as I did so, I presented him with a small statue of Our Lady of the Snows.

I also told him that, through the Oblates' and lay employees' ministry at the Missionary Association in Belleville, we have distributed over nine million rosaries to people all over the world. As I told him this, he smiled slightly and said, "Yes, I know the Oblates!"

Archbishop John Harvey, an American prelate who directs papal traffic at these weekly audiences, pulled me aside as I got up to leave the Holy Father.

"This must be a very proud moment for you," he gushed.

As Oblate Director of the Missionary Association, it has been my privilege to travel to some of the places where the Oblates are ministering in various parts of the world. Not only was I finally able to visit more of Iowa and the Midwest, I was fortunate to travel to Brazil, South Africa, Madagascar, Haiti, Sri Lanka, Lesotho and some of the beautiful shrines in Europe to see firsthand the ministry of the Oblates.

My travels were enriching insofar as they taught me a lot about various cultures, religions, habits, customs, and diverse people. The Oblates, often originally from a different country and culture from where they are ministering, have adapted themselves to a totally new way of living.

I admired how resourceful and innovative these Oblates were, as well as the sacrifices they have made to leave what is familiar and modern to what is sometimes strange and outmoded.

BRAZIL

I traveled to central Brazil in 1994 with Bill Magrath, a photographer at the Missionary Association, and visited some of the favellas, i.e., the impoverished neighborhoods, that comprise a good part of the large parish community where the Oblates minister there.

As Fr. Pete Curran, O.M.I., and I walked from house to house, meeting his parishioners, I was edified by the generosity and welcoming spirit of these poor people. They have so little but their spirit is undaunting and infectious. They were quick to offer a cup of coffee, a small bowl of rice, some beans or bread.

Father Pete and I had been walking and visiting for a couple hours when it began to rain, first just a drizzle but then much harder and more intense. I was enjoying our visits very much, appreciating how gracious the people were and especially how much they enjoyed having Fr. Pete stop by.

Father Pete mentioned, a couple of times, that we should now go back to the rectory.

"I'm fine to stay," I told him. "I'm really

enjoying this."

"Yes, but when it rains hard like this, the open sewers flood and many of the sewer rats have nowhere to go and will be running along our path," he said.

"You're absolutely right, Pete," I said. "Let's go home."

He grinned widely and we quickly made our way back to the rectory.

I vividly remembered the large rats I would see when we shelled corn when I was a young boy. These rats had been eating corn in the crib all winter and some of them looked as large as dogs to me.

Dad would call out to me, "Louis, kill that rat," as it quickly scampered away.

I would think to myself, "Yeah, right, dad." And I would stand there, frozen, too afraid to even move, much less try to kill the rat.

When I visited Brazil in 2004 with my sister Suzanne, along with Bill Magrath and Bernadette McCaffrey at the Missionary Association, I visited Fr. Ed Figueroa, O.M.I., and the community of children he has taken off the streets to live with him as family.

Father Ed is insistent about the philosophy of his family: "This is not an orphanage, not even just a community. It is a family and these children are brothers and sisters for each other, even though most of them are not related to each other. We teach the older, healthier ones to help the younger, more infirm ones to get dressed, prepare meals, get ready for school, do homework, clean, wash dishes."

The older, healthier children certainly have their work

cut out for them because Fr. Ed has intentionally taken the physically infirm, and the physically and mentally handicapped children from the streets to live with him.

"They are the ones who would be more likely to die sooner," he explained to me. "There is no way they would be able to last on the streets."

Father Ed proudly told me that his monthly grocery list includes, "approximately," he says with a wink, 343 gallons of milk, 112 dozen eggs, 374 pounds of rice, 374 pounds of beans and 4,200 rolls. In addition, many of these children have special needs because of their disabilities.

Because the government of Brazil does very little to educate children with disabilities, he established a school precisely for this purpose. The school is called *Guardian Angels.* There is no tuition because Fr. Ed does not want anyone turned away because of lack of funds. It is Fr. Ed's way of helping the many children with disabilities receive a formal education.

There is an unusually high number of children with physical and mental disabilities because of the very poor nutrition in Brazil. Many of these children have to fend for themselves on the streets.

One of Fr. Ed's "kids" was a small boy who had been shut up in an abandoned hut for nearly three weeks. When the child was discovered, he was so extremely malnourished that the authorities didn't think he would survive the trip to the hospital. Miraculously, the boy recovered. Soon after, the doctor brought him to the only place and person he knew would be willing to help: Fr. Ed Figueroa, O.M.I.

Today that small child has a name: Allan. He is one of the many abandoned children who received a gift that he could have never imagined: a place to call home. As God has adopted each one of us as His sons and daughters, so Fr. Ed has adopted these children and given them ready-made brothers and sisters.

Father Ed also explained to me that many of his older children now help him serve the needy people of the neighborhood.

My sister Suzanne and I, along with Bill and Bernadette, went with him and some of his family to distribute corn chowder to the poor. At each place we went, people were lined up to receive a couple scoops of this sweet soup. Suzanne and I had tasted it earlier; we both hated it. Most importantly, however, the Brazilians loved it!

Father Ed said a quick prayer at each place, knowing the people in line were anxious to get a few mouths full. Many were kind enough to bring an extra container for a sick parent or relative back home. Some had walked a considerable distance to receive this nourishment.

Father Ed later explained that for many who had come, this would be their only meal that day.

It was quite uncomfortable spooning out the chowder in the heat and humidity of a Brazilian summer afternoon. Seeing the joy on the peoples' faces as I ladled the hot soup into their containers helped me forget about my own lack of comfort. Seeing their faces as they ate some of the sweet chowder was more than enough thanks for all of us.

One young lady named Carmelia had taken dancing

lessons and now she spends much of her time teaching dancing to the children in Fr. Ed's family. It was delightful to see such a talented young girl giving back to others a talent she had learned. Carmelia had been in desperate need of Fr. Ed's help years before. Her mother, years before, in a fit of rage had thrown boiling water on her. This was not the first time she had been abused. Father Ed said that when he first laid eyes on her, she was so disfigured he could barely make out her features. There was a strong sense of family being built by Fr. Ed among these children.

Sometimes a child is simply left at Fr. Ed's doorstep because people know that he cannot say "no."

This Oblate charism and love for the poor is not only present in Brazil but also over three thousand miles away in Ukraine.

UKRAINE

Oblate Father Radoslaw Zmitrowicz ministers to the people in the town of Slavutych which is the town closest to Chernobyl, site of the nuclear power plant disaster in 1986.

In 2001, I visited him with my sister Suzanne and two employees, a writer and a photographer, from the Missionary Association.

Father Rad was struggling to build a new church, with minimal funds available. The house where he stays is so small that he cannot accommodate guests.

Refusing to turn us away, he quickly threw some

blankets on a couple church pews which became our open bedroom in the new church loft.

My singing talent has never been an envy to anyone but my sister Suzanne and I can now proudly say we were in the church choir!

The nuclear accident caused radioactive material to contaminate a large area near Chernobyl. More than 130,000 people had to evacuate their homes immediately after the disaster. Estimates put the number of people who have experienced health problems because of Chernobyl at 600,000. Many have high rates of leukemia and tumors and many children are born with illnesses that doctors are unable to identify.

Father Radoslaw lives on contaminated soil and eats contaminated food. Several of the Oblates in Ukraine told me they experience nose bleeds often, coughing spells, and breathing difficulties as a direct result of the contaminated air.

Breathing this contaminated air is a particular problem for Fr. Rad since he had previously suffered from a bout of tuberculosis, a condition from which he has never fully recovered.

Despite it all, he keeps his humor.

One night as we were eating dinner, my sister Suzanne commented about the large, round vegetables in the bowl on the table in front of her.

"What are they, Father? They look like delicious red cabbages," she said to Fr. Rad.

"Oh, no, those are Chernobyl cherries," he said, completely serious.

And then, a few seconds later, all the while

completely enjoying the frozen look on our faces, he gave his usual hearty laugh.

For the past several years, Fr. Rad and his fellow Oblates have organized trips for children to spend some time outside of the contaminated area, usually taking them to Poland. Doctors have told the Oblates that these holidays allow the youngsters' lungs to recover a bit from the effects of radiation poisoning. When they return, they have less difficulty breathing and more energy.

If Ukraine is the most contaminated country where the Oblates minister, a strong case could be made that Haiti is one of the poorest countries where they minister.

HAITI

I will never forget my visit to *St. Etienne Home for the Elderly* in Haiti. I went there in 1999 with a writer and a photographer from the Missionary Association.

On the afternoon we visited, most of the 38 residents were seated in a screened-in hallway that overlooks a yard. The home is very modest and there are three residents in each small room. The oldest resident is 99 and the youngest is 44. Ten of the 38 are blind. They would likely be begging on the streets if it were not for *St. Etienne Home*. Quite possibly, they would not even be alive. It's hard to imagine anyone surviving long, begging on the streets of Haiti.

One woman, Emilina, offered me her chair. I was moved by her kind gesture. Even though she had little to give, she wanted to share something with me. I was reluctant to accept her kind offer but she was insistent. This was typical of the poor I have encountered in my visits to Third World Countries; they are anxious to share the little they have, even the last of what they have.

The Missionary Oblates provide for *St. Etienne Home.* It costs about $18,000 to operate the home per year. That is a shoestring budget, especially considering there are only eight workers there who care for the residents.

Oblate Father Francis Mitchell was ministering at this home. When I visited there, he had already been ministering there several years. He was certainly qualified to work with the elderly, since he himself was 83 at the time! He felt he could not retire because he was helping with some of the administrative duties of the home. He celebrated Mass for them on Sundays and visited the residents once or twice a week, besides. Father Francis was having trouble getting around himself. He has pain in his feet and legs and needs a walker to get around.

At the end of our week there, traveling all over the island, Fr. Joe Corriveau, O.M.I., our capable driver, invited us back sometime.

"We don't get that many visitors here," he said.

I was brutally honest with him. "I don't know, Joe, this has been a rough week."

He gave a slight, knowing smile. On the plane back to the U.S. I thought about what I had said and felt guilty about it. My comment probably didn't surprise him too much, knowing as he does the tremendous life style difference between Haiti and the United States.

The Oblates certainly are very aware they are making a difference. The healing and the hope they are bringing to these people continues to give them enthusiasm and a vibrant spirit.

Several of the U.S. Oblates who have ministered in Haiti are at an age when they could return to the U.S. to retire. But the majority of them remain in Haiti because they want to stay close to the people whom they have served all their lives. They would be able to retire to the U.S. in much more comfortable conditions but instead many of them choose to live in this very modest retirement facility in Haiti.

After their afternoon naps, these retired Oblates sit on their front porch, anxiously awaiting the many people walking home from work who go out of their way to stop by this retirement home and spend some time in conversation. They are obviously grateful to these Oblates for the many years of service and ministry given to them and to their families. The Haitians are grateful that these Oblates remain here with them, even in retirement.

Now, these hardworking Haitians show the Oblates they are able to offer back in thanks to them some lively conversation, a joke or two and genuine concern about their health and well-being.

Seeing the tender care of these Haitians for the elder Oblates was a very touching moment for me. I became quite emotional seeing the love and care the Haitians are anxious to give back to these Oblates in thanks for so many years of generous service.

I also visited Sri Lanka, the small island off the southeast coast of India where the Oblates have been ministering since 1846, being sent there by the Founder himself, St. Eugene De Mazenod.

Shortly after I arrived, the Oblates drove me from Colombo, the capital city, to the Shrine of Our Lady of the Rosary, in the northern part of the country. It is an Oblate Shrine, very popular with the people of Sri Lanka.

I was pleased to be given a tour of the Shrine by Fr. Jeevendra Paul, O.M.I., former Provincial, of the Province of Jaffna. As he proudly showed me some of the devotional sites, we stopped as we approached the devotional site of Our Lady of Lourdes.

"I think you have a devotional site of Our Lady of Lourdes at the Shrine of Our Lady of the Snows in Belleville, do you not?" he asked.

"Yes, we do," I responded, "in fact, it is the most popular site on our Shrine grounds."

As I continued to stand in front of their Shrine of Our Lady of Lourdes with him, we spoke about the many ministries of the approximately 170 Oblates on this tiny island country. Suddenly, I noticed something missing.

"I don't see a statue of St. Bernadette," I exclaimed, just now noticing that the statue of the Blessed Mother was looking downward but to no one.

"Oh, I forget to tell people anymore since it happened so long ago. We had a herd of elephants come stomping through the Shrine and they destroyed the statue of St. Bernadette," he said, somewhat ashamedly.

Hearing that, I thought, well, that's one problem I haven't had to deal with at our Shrine in Belleville!

Father Paul continued to tell me about some of the events and activities the Oblates promote at this Shrine. He said that the Oblates invite people of many faith traditions of the world to the Shrine of Our Lady of the Rosary: Hindus, Muslims, Buddhists and Christians to come together and dialog in mutual respect and understanding, to learn from each other, to more deeply appreciate one another's faith traditions, cultures and backgrounds.

I wondered quietly to myself: could September 11th, 2001, have been avoided if more of this kind of dialog had taken place in our world, and if there was more appreciation of the faith traditions and cultures of the peoples of the world?

Organizations like the United Nations haven't been very successful bringing people of different cultures, faiths or political views to the peace table.

The Oblates, however, were somehow able to bring about these important connections.

The Shrine of Our Lady of the Snows has also done this kind of ministry quite successfully with its interfaith programs and through the annual Festival of Faiths and Cultures. Certainly more of this is needed in our world.

The Oblates also were instrumental in helping the government of Sri Lanka negotiate an end to nineteen years of civil war. Father Seamus Finn, an American Oblate, and Fr. Oswald Firth, a Sri Lankan Oblate, helped bring the warring tribes to the peace table for negotiations.

More recently, the tribes are again at war.

Membership among the Oblates themselves in Sri Lanka comes from both of the tribal warring factions so it was logical for the Oblates to be part of the negotiating process.

The Oblates built huts for the many visitors to Our Lady of the Rosary Shrine in northern Sri Lanka. Because travel to the Shrine was difficult, pilgrims often needed an overnight place to stay when they visited the Shrine.

When the civil war broke out, the Oblates knew that many of the people who were displaced from their homes had nowhere to go. The Oblates agreed to allow many of these displaced people to stay on the Shrine grounds in these huts.

Here they received three meals a day, a place to stay where they would be safe and the opportunity to receive the Sacraments daily. They also could take advantage of the counseling and spiritual direction the Oblates were able to provide.

Some of these people told me they had been forced to move as many as seven times before finally settling at the Shrine.

Many of them cried as they told me about their gratitude to the Oblates for offering them a safe haven. The Oblates promised them that they could stay at the Shrine in complete safety until the civil war ended.

These people were happy to stay at the Shrine with hardly any of their possessions because here, at least, they lived in relative peace and security.

MADAGASCAR

As I reflected on the work of the Oblates in such places as Haiti and Sri Lanka, I was certain I had visited some of the poorest places where the Oblates minister.

In Haiti, almost everyone is poor because there is no sound infrastructure in the country. Madagascar has this same kind of dire poverty for the same reason.

For five days in August 2001, I had the opportunity to travel there and visit some of our Oblate missions. I went there with a writer and a photographer from the Missionary Association.

Madagascar is an island country, located off the southeast coast of Africa. While in Madagascar, I traveled with a young Polish Oblate named Fr. Klaudiusz Hermanski.

We started out early one morning to drive to the Oblate seminary where young men are studying to become Oblate priests and Brothers. The travel distance that would have taken us perhaps four hours on our highways here in the United States took twelve hours there. Along the way, we stopped to visit with many gracious, smiling people — but very poor people.

They were working in the rice fields or carrying a large basket on their head while walking along the road or operating a small roadside stand, always ready to make a sale. No matter what they were doing, they loved for us to stop to chat. Their wide smiles were infectious. They always took time to speak with us.

Most of the people there live very simply and grow much of what they need to eat — rice, potatoes, carrots.

Father Klaudiusz told me that most people there have an income of about $200 a year.

A group of five Oblates arrived in Madagascar in 1980. When they arrived, they met with many difficulties — the weather was extremely hot, and the lack of good roads made traveling very difficult. These Oblates came from Poland, so they had to first learn the language and the culture.

When I visited in 2001, there were twenty-five Oblate priests there and five Oblate Brothers. Forty-five young men were studying to become Brothers and priests.

This says a lot about our Oblate missionaries in Madagascar. They work hard to train young people who will continue to help meet the needs of the poor there for many years.

Father Marian Lis was another Oblate I met. He took me to a very poor neighborhood where the Oblates plan to build a community center. Already, some Oblate seminarians are working in this area, teaching young children the alphabet and the Catholic Faith. For many in this area, this community center will help provide medical supplies, food, drinking water and a place for the people to gather.

During my visit, I also went to a leprosarium. It is hard to believe that in this day and age, people still contract leprosy — but they do, and I saw some young people whose hands and feet were deformed because of this horrible disease. One gentleman I met had lost both his feet and lower legs to leprosy.

As I was leaving the leprosarium, one of the Sisters who works there reminded me to wash my hands. I stood at the sink, scrubbing and scrubbing with the soap she provided. After about five minutes of this, she gently said, "I think your hands are clean enough now." I felt somewhat embarrassed to be so concerned about my own health in the midst of such senseless illness and poverty. She must have thought that I was making sure not to leave with any of the leprosy on my hands!

In fact, I need not have worried. Only the poor whose immune system is quite weak are prone to contract this horrible disease.

I also visited a hospital where I was able to pray with some of the patients there. I can tell you it bore little resemblance to the hospitals here in the United States. There was no modern medical equipment, and the furnishings I saw were quite old.

Oblates in Madagascar also travel to remote areas to meet with people and to celebrate Mass. Were it not for these Oblates, many people would not have the opportunity to receive the Sacraments.

Even though our mission in Madagascar is relatively new, the Oblates there have already accomplished much by opening a scholasticate, a house where Oblates study to become priests, which has been supported by our donors here in the United States.

In Madagascar, it costs only $20 a month to feed, clothe, and care for a child. Not even a dollar a day. The survival of many of these children depends on the goodwill of people beyond the shores of this impoverished country.

Seventy percent of the people in Madagascar cannot read or write, not even their own name.

LESOTHO

In southwestern Africa lies the small, landlocked, mountainous country of Lesotho.

Of all the Oblate missions in 70 countries worldwide, I believe our missions in Lesotho are quite unique. The word "Lesotho" means "Kingdom in the Sky."

I proudly reflected on the fact that Lesotho is very likely the single country, of all the countries where the Oblates minister, where the Oblates have had the greatest impact. That is because every Catholic mission in Lesotho — literally every church, school, and community outreach program was established by the Missionary Oblates.

The Oblate most known for his ministry in Lesotho is Blessed Joseph Gerard, who lived from 1831 to 1914. Known as the spiritual father of the people of Lesotho, Fr. Gerard continues to be well-loved, and the people of Lesotho continue to pray for his intercession in their lives.

Pope John Paul II visited Lesotho in 1988, and beatified Fr. Gerard. That day was a very special occasion for the people of Lesotho.

Blessed Gerard's grave is in a small stone church and people often visit there and pray for their needs.

Another site dedicated to this great missionary is called the Cave of Blessed Joseph Gerard. This cave-like setting is in a small valley where local people took refuge during warfare against the Boers. Father Gerard was with the people on one of those occasions. The Boers were shooting down into the valley from the surrounding heights. Father Gerard was saying his Breviary when a bullet went through the small book but missed him.

In August 1999, I visited this tiny, beautiful country. While I was there, the Oblates celebrated the 75th anniversary of St. Augustine's Seminary, founded and staffed by the Oblates. This was a wonderful celebration with alumni visiting from all parts of Lesotho and several other African countries. Dignitaries and people from the community also attended the day-long celebration. The outdoor Eucharistic Liturgy lasted almost three hours. With the colorful costumes, the melodious chanting and the vibrant dancing, the time passed quickly. After the liturgy, seminarians as well as groups of lay people performed more songs and dances.

This seminary educates men and women of Lesotho and other African countries who have been called to priesthood, Brotherhood and Sisterhood. There were thirty-eight Oblate seminarians attending classes at St. Augustine's and living in community at the Oblate seminary. I was edified to see so many young men answering the call to become Oblates of Mary Immaculate.

During my visit, I stayed at the seminary, and I spent some time with the seminarians. These young men work hard at their studies and show great commitment to their vocation. Each morning, the seminarians join in prayer at Mass. Even at 8:00 a.m., these spirited young men rejoiced in their faith by singing and playing musical instruments.

Another important ministry of the Oblates has been the National University of Lesotho. Day-to-day operations of this university have been turned over to the state, but the Oblates play an important role in campus ministry. For many years, during apartheid, this university was the only place of higher education for Blacks in southern Africa.

My fellow Oblate, Father Alexander Montanyane, was ministering to the university's students. Father Montanyane had been involved with a new project for the Oblates — the official opening of a Catholic FM radio station. At the opening ceremony, the Bishops of Lesotho gave this message:

"From the beginning, the Church in Lesotho started teaching people to read and write, it built them schools, health centers and other development projects...all in order to pursue its mission of proclaiming the Good News of salvation."

Father Montanyane added that "the principal objective of the radio station will be to communicate the Good News of the Kingdom to all..."

The Oblates also are responsible for much of the printed material in Lesotho. The Oblates publish several newspapers, textbooks and missals. These materials — printed in English — help the people of Lesotho learn and worship together.

Like other countries in Africa, the AIDS epidemic is affecting the lives of many in Lesotho. And again, one of the major focuses for the Oblates is education. Oblate Father Augustinus Bane, then Provincial of Lesotho, spoke at the International AIDS Conference held in South Africa. He gave this compassionate plea to those attending the conference and to people across the world:

"I believe we must be a Church which presents HIV/AIDS education programs and home-based care and counseling, which are in accordance with gospel values and our moral ideas. But we must also be a Church which can speak a word of hope and enlightenment, a word which touches the heart of the matter for people who are facing profound human challenges and are struggling to cope with the reality of living and dying with AIDS."

The Oblates in Lesotho offer words of hope and enlightenment to the people there everyday.

During my visit to Lesotho, I noticed that it is a very young country. I saw many children and young adults. And for these young people, life is not always what we would hope for them. While many children in Lesotho do have the opportunity to go to school, many others must spend much of the year working to help earn some income for their families.

In many families, young boys are responsible for caring for the family's herd of goats or sheep. Because of the country's rocky terrain, these shepherd boys must walk long distances, leading their herd to find new grazing land. These boys may be gone from their families for months at a time. They carry their blankets and food with them and stay overnight in small shacks which are built in the countryside. For my fellow Oblates in Lesotho, an important focus will be to reach out to young people like these shepherd boys and share with them the Good News of God's love.

Lourdes, France

There is no place on this earth like Lourdes. I say this with a firm conviction because nowhere else have I witnessed people so proud about their faith and so willing to express it so openly.

For several years, I traveled to Lourdes to take with me the petitions, the prayers of our donors. I was only too happy to do so.

I first went to Lourdes in February 1998, with the prayer requests of our donors in hand to place them in the petition box at the Sacred Grotto.

I expected there would be some mysterious magic about Lourdes and maybe for some there is but it wasn't the kind of magic I expected.

The number of miraculous cures attributed to Our Lady's intercession at Lourdes is under 100 since the apparition of Our Lady to Bernadette Soubirous in 1858. There may be many more miracles that have occurred but the official number of miracles verified by the Vatican is quite small. Yet, over five million pilgrims continue to visit there each year.

People travel to Lourdes on pilgrimage to pray. Even people with dramatic physical handicaps by and large told me they come to Lourdes to pray — for deeper faith, pray to accept what comes their way, pray for greater understanding of God's — and Our Lady's — power and presence in their lives.

This was a great surprise to me. I thought Lourdes was about miraculous, incredible cures. This was what I assumed people prayed for there; this was why they traveled there and if the cure wasn't received, they went home with great disappointment and frustration.

I'm sure there are some who travel to Lourdes with that intent. But that wasn't what was on the minds and in the hearts of the pilgrims I met.

They came to Lourdes to accept their particular situation, to grow in faith, to understand more deeply how God is working in their lives and to ask Our Lady's intercession for a sick mother, a grieving cousin, an infirmed uncle, most often someone other than their own needs.

I was under the impression that they came to Lourdes to tell God and Our Lady what was their agenda, their plan, their will. This couldn't have been further from what I encountered there.

The people I met came there with tremendous openness, deep faith, untiring trust that they might accept God's will and way in their lives.

I felt the same kind of peace there that I felt in the cemetery at St. Henry's Seminary.

Like me, everyone else, it seems, who goes to Lourdes wants to make immediate plans to return there again.

It's a place where Our Lady grabs hold of you and doesn't let go.

UNITED STATES

In the United States, a primary focus of the Oblates' ministry has been the growing Hispanic population. The

Oblates minister with the Hispanic people located in big cities and small towns in many parts of the country.

Just a few hours' drive north of the Mexican border, the Oblates have formed a special faith community in the San Fernando Valley of California. Three parishes — Santa Rosa, Mary Immaculate, and St. Ferdinand — are served by one group of Oblates in a tri-parish community.

When I was Vocation Director for the Oblates in the mid-90's, I visited these parishes to see firsthand the work of the Oblates there and to meet with the other Vocation Directors.

We had planned to go out to dinner Saturday evening at 7:00 p.m. to set our agenda for our days of meetings together.

Father Tom Rush, O.M.I., was our host. He was ministering at the parishes there and had planned to take us to dinner. The seven o'clock hour came and went and even the eight o'clock hour. At 8:30 p.m., Fr. Tom walked into the rectory, profusely apologetic about the late hour of his arrival, explaining to us that he was counseling some parishioners, after hearing confessions, after celebrating Mass.

Father Tom told us at dinner that he had celebrated four Masses that day, heard confessions for a couple hours and counseled parishioners for three hours. "This was pretty much a normal Saturday," he said.

Among the three parishes, there may be as many as seventy five baptisms on any given weekend, as well as eight to ten weddings. In addition, the three parishes celebrate a total of twenty four Masses each weekend.

The Oblates support a scholarship fund and a credit

union to help new parishioners adjust to life in the United States. In addition, we provide space for classes and testing to help those who want to become naturalized citizens.

In Brownsville, Texas, the Oblates have been serving the poor for more than 150 years. The first Oblates arrived in Brownsville on horseback and established missions along the Rio Grande River.

At that time, most of the people living in this desolate part of Texas were not Catholic. However, they were delighted to receive the gospel.

The Oblates made lengthy pastoral trips on horseback, visiting ranches to instruct children and adults and administer the Sacraments. They celebrated Mass on crude altars lovingly decorated with needlework and wild flowers. They became known as "The Cavalry of Christ."

These early Oblates in Brownsville had to endure many hardships, from disease to attacks by bandits. Yellow fever alone claimed the lives of eight of them.

Today, the Oblates continue to serve the needy of south Texas. They provide food and clothing to people down on their luck and sponsor programs to help people learn English.

Another center of Hispanic ministry for the Oblates is south Florida. In Miami, the Oblates are ministering to immigrants from all parts of Latin America. One of the best examples of our work is St. Monica Parish.

In the hallways at the parish school, students can be found conversing in English, Spanish, French and an assortment of dialects. Teachers at the school come from a variety of areas including Puerto Rico, Columbia, Cuba and Jamaica.

"We have a very unique little place here," said school principal, Manuel Felix Varela. "It is amazing how the kids blend so well together. Nobody ever feels like they are odd because of where their family comes from.

In Lowell, Massachusetts, the Oblates took the unusual step of changing the entire focus of a parish, including its name, to better serve a growing Hispanic population there.

In 1868, the Oblates established St. Jean-Baptiste Parish in Lowell to serve the French Canadians who were working in the city's textile mills. Years later, when French-speaking residents began moving to the suburbs, the parish population dropped dramatically, forcing the church to close for a few years.

The Oblates then decided to refocus their ministry in the community. Wanting to reach out to the growing Hispanic population in Lowell, the Oblates reopened the church and renamed it *Nuestra Senora Del Carmen*.

The revitalized parish was one of the first in the Archdiocese of Boston to celebrate Eucharistic Liturgies in Spanish. People from throughout northern Massachusetts and southern New Hampshire began flocking to the parish.

Closer to home, at the Shrine of Our Lady of the Snows, Fr. Raul Salas, O.M.I., the Associate Director, was instrumental in establishing a Hispanic ministry program. Noticing that a growing number of Hispanic pilgrims were making visits to the Shrine, he developed programs and events to help serve their needs.

Father Raul further convinced me to build a replica of Tepeyac Hill at the Shrine.

"If you build, they will come," he told me.

Tepeyac Hill is the site of the Blessed Mother's apparition to Juan Diego in the mid 1500's, near Mexico City.

One of the special events at the Shrine is a sunrise service, followed by Mass, held on December 12th, the Feast of Our Lady of Guadalupe. Another major event in honor of Our Lady of Guadalupe is held each year on the first Sunday of September. The day begins with Mass followed by a festive lunch with a visit to Tepeyac Hill. This is a full day of dancing, singing and celebration of their faith and culture.

Father Raul was right: we have built and they continue to come.

My brother Oblates in New Orleans responded quickly to the devastation of Hurricane Katrina which crashed into the shores of the Gulf Coast on August 29, 2005. Katrina brought winds of over 160 m.p.h.

Stories of the tragedy were quickly spread throughout the country, but many stories were left untold.

Father Mike Amesse, O.M.I., along with Fr. Tony Rigoli, O.M.I., were at the Oblate Shrine of St. Jude in New Orleans when the storm hit.

"It was apocalyptic," said Fr. Mike. "Suddenly, New Orleans became a Third World Country. You could see people in the streets, stranded, with a look of utter hopelessness. You could see it in their eyes."

Through constant communication with the police station across the street from the Shrine, the Oblates began to understand the severity of the situation. They decided to flee. A police officer drove them to the river, and they left New Orleans on foot. Fortunately, they received assistance from two Jesuits at a retreat house.

They gave Fr. Mike and Fr. Tony a car, which they used to drive to an Oblate retreat house near Houston, Texas, where they arrived on Friday, September 2.

"It felt so good to make it to the retreat house. I was happy to finally be in a safe place," explained Fr. Mike.

Father Mike soon learned that many other refugees were arriving in Houston, just ten miles away from the retreat house.

"We switched gears quickly. At first, I wanted to pick up some food and water and bring it back to the people who needed it in New Orleans. But when we found out about all the other refugees here, we knew they needed our help."

Father Mike, Fr. Tony, and Brother Profirio Garcia, O.M.I., traveled back and forth daily into Houston to provide support and spiritual presence to the survivors.

Later, Fr. Mike was able to report, "The atmosphere is very positive. Things are well organized. People are receiving clothes, good food, and there are plenty of doctors for people who need assistance."

A five-minute drive from the Shrine of Our Lady of the Snows lies the city of East St. Louis, Illinois. This impoverished city lies in the shadow of the Shrine.

The demographics tell the story. Thirty-one percent of families are below the poverty line, including nearly fifty percent of children under the age of 18.

Twenty-five percent of people over the age of 65 live in poverty.

East St. Louis has been referred to as "the most distressed small city in America." Because of its extreme poverty levels, the Oblates, in conjunction with Catholic Urban Programs (CUP), strive to bring life and security back to the people of this river town.

In an enormous web of ministry, the Oblates and CUP provide soup kitchens, medical and financial assistance, family counseling and safe shelter to the needy of East St. Louis. Brother Ed Driggens, O.M.I., who volunteers his time with CUP said, "I really enjoy being down here. It's another example of the Oblates working with the poor."

CUP is not the only program that the Oblates work with to bring a bit of charity and joy to the deprived people living in this small town. Holy Angels' Shelter is a haven of safety and service, protecting battered women and children from the harsh realities of living in East St. Louis. The shelter helps uprooted families move on with their lives by providing new jobs and new homes to those in need. Holy Angels also works in conjunction with local churches to provide food and necessities to families throughout the year, including gifts for children during the Christmas season.

The generosity of volunteers working with these programs helps to improve the lives of these underprivileged people. With financial support, prayers and Brother Ed's assistance, the Oblates continue to nurture and encourage the seeds of hope to flourish for the people of East St. Louis.

For more than sixty years, donors to the Missionary Association in Belleville and Oblate Missions in San Antonio have given generously to the worldwide ministries of the Missionary Oblates of Mary Immaculate.

Generous monetary gifts and an abundance of prayers have helped 4,500 Oblate Brothers and priests serve the poor in over 70 countries around the world. The Oblates feed the hungry in Brazil, take in the orphaned in Sri Lanka, form community in Madagascar.

One place the Oblates and their benefactors have helped is Sisseton, South Dakota. In this rural town, built on an open Native American reservation, Oblates serve both Native and European Americans.

This town, struggling with prejudice, unemployment, and poverty, has battled two disasters recently. With the help of our donors and the Oblates, both challenges have been met head on and overcome.

In the early morning hours of September 21, 2005, an arsonist started a fire in the altar server's sacristy of the Oblate St. Peter's Church in Sisseton, South Dakota. The Pastor, Fr. Norman Volk, O.M.I., reported that the fire traveled along a wall to the sacristy on the opposite side of the church. The church suffered major damage before the fire was brought under control.

Soon after the devastating fire, a 17-year-old youth confessed to the horrific crime. He admitted that he first broke into the Boys' and Girls' Club and stole candy, leaving a trail of candy wrappers. He then broke into St. Peter's Church, where he not only started a fire, but managed to dislodge the Tabernacle from its base and throw it to the floor; he also overturned flower vases and the Paschal Candle.

For years, St. Peter's had been the cornerstone of the congregation. It was the place where children were baptized, received First Holy Communion, and were confirmed. Marriage ceremonies and funeral Masses were celebrated there. Members came together to worship as one faith community. After the fire, only memories remained of the church.

"When I prepared my homily for Mass a week after the fire, it felt like I was preparing for a funeral," said Fr. Walter Butor, O.M.I., Associate Pastor of St. Peter's. "I felt like God's house, my house, [the town's] house, had been violated."

The parish was devastated, but in early 2006, the Oblates learned that they would be able to repair the present structure of the church without having to build a completely new church. Greatly relieved by this news, Fr. Norman and Fr. Butor gathered with their community to find a way to rebuild their beloved church.

After sixteen months, the parishioners of St. Peters finally had their church again, and celebrated a rededication on January 14, 2007.

The other disaster took place on November 26, 2005, when an ice storm barreled its way into Sisseton. "I've heard of severe storm warnings," Fr. Butor said, "but never blizzard warnings. And that's what we had — a blizzard."

Ice and snow pummeled the town, with winds recorded at about 40 m.p.h. with gusts well over 60 m.p.h. The intense weather blew over trees, which took out power lines. Half the town was without heat or electricity. Roads were shut down and connections to nearby towns were blocked. The townspeople were trapped. Once again, Sisseton was in turmoil. Was its faith strong enough to battle another challenge?

Fathers Butor and Volk set up a make-shift shelter in St. Catherine's Parish Hall. Fifty people camped out on the gym floor.

"It's a good place to be because it has heat, running water and bathrooms," Fr. Butor explained.

The National Guard brought in sleeping cots; the tribe supplied food. Volunteers stayed with the people and cooked for them.

To help fight off the chill, Fr. Butor passed out handmade star quilts.

For years, donors to the Missionary Association of Mary Immaculate had been sending their prayer requests with a donation to the Missionary Association, and these requests were placed on stars of fabric and then these stars were sewn together by Native Americans into star quilts. The quilts were then sent to the reservation, and the people of Sisseton prayed for those intentions. Father Butor gave away about thirty-five quilts to those living in the parish hall.

As the people of Sisseton wrapped themselves in these blankets, they were also wrapping themselves in the prayers and support from many generous donors to the Oblates of Mary Immaculate.

Seeing firsthand the exciting ministries of the Oblates in so many places in the world made me proud to be listed among their number.

I could heartily agree with Pope Pius XI's statement about the Oblates, "specialists in difficult missions."

I understood why Pope John Paul II, even in his frailty when I visited him in 2004, could so readily proclaim, "I know the Oblates!"

The Missionary Oblates of Mary Immaculate are known — and loved — by many, in many parts of the world.

Saint Eugene De Mazenod chose as the motto of the Missionary Oblates, "He has sent me to preach the gospel to the poor. The poor have the gospel preached to them."

This task, to evangelize, to preach the gospel, is the key to the Missionary Oblates' presence all over the world. All else plays second fiddle to this focus.

I have been proud to see firsthand in so many varied circumstances and countries, that we have remained faithful to the mission given to us by St. Eugene almost two hundred years ago.

Chapter Thirteen:
Life Is Difficult, Even for Iowans

The first three words of M. Scott Peck's popular book, *The Road Less Traveled,* are: "Life is difficult."

There has not been a human being created who has not experienced, in a personal way, this phenomenon. Life is indeed difficult, at some time or other, for each one of us.

Perhaps some of the reason we often find life so difficult is due to our misperceived expectations.

If I enjoy good health most of my life and then break my leg and need to use crutches for a period of time, I can easily become discouraged and angry. My leg served me well for so many years so now that it is broken and I cannot properly use it, I am disappointed and frustrated.

What would my attitude be if my approach were this: all of life is gift, the use of my legs for so many years has been a gift, and gifts are freely given. I don't deserve these gifts; I did nothing to earn them. Thus, when the use of one of these gifts is no longer possible, I don't view the lack of use as something less or as a diminishment.

Perhaps my approach could be: I never deserved the healthy use of the leg in the first place. And rather than concentrating on the leg that I now cannot use, I decide to focus on the many other gifts I have been given.

This reasoning can sound easy; living it is quite a different matter.

No one of us has done anything to deserve our health, for example. No one of us can earn our health. No one owes it to us. Therefore, our health, our environment, relationships in our lives, having meaning in life, seeing our grandchildren grow, all of these are gifts.

Focusing on the positive, i.e., the gifts we have and enjoy, rather than the ones that we might one day no longer be able to use properly, can make a huge difference in our attitude and in our acceptance of what comes our way.

All that we are — and have — is a gift from God. Gifts are not deserved or even earned. They are purely the result of God's love and generosity.

My parents died within four months of each other in 1996; dad, from the effects of a stroke, in August and mom, from a weakened heart, in December.

It was certainly very difficult for me, and for my brothers and sisters, to accept the fact that in such a short time both of them were gone.

I received a note of condolence from Francis Cardinal George, O.M.I., the Archbishop of Chicago, when my mother died.

How kind of this man to write me, I thought. Certainly he has an extremely busy schedule so I felt honored that he took the time to write to me. He expressed the usual condolences, proper for such an occasion. His last paragraph of the brief note at first angered me.

"Stay with your pain," he wrote.

I didn't understand his message and it seemed harsh and uncaring, yet I knew that he must have had good reason for expressing himself this way.

Giving myself permission to grieve, focusing in on my feelings about the circumstances of their deaths, remembering who they were for me and how they impacted my life, what they taught me and how they loved me, has helped me move on, but never forget. Staying with my pain, giving myself to the process of grieving, later allowed me to move on.

Cardinal George had given me good insight into the grieving process.

Part of that grieving process has been to study some of their physical characteristics in my own, traits of each of their personalities in my own, a desire and hunger for God which they both had, in my own life.

In my own life, I hope I can continue to honor their lives by embracing the patience and the service and the care which they showed me and my brothers and sisters.

In each of my brothers and sisters, I do see

particular gifts and virtues of my mom and dad that manifest themselves in a special way:

June – service

Carolyn – honesty

Suzanne – loyalty

David – generosity

Muriel – caring

Elmer – balance

I see that each one of them is an extension of mom and dad, a continuing sign of mom and dad's presence in the world. Each one of us, their children, continues their presence in the world in and through the gifts and virtues they passed on to us. In short, we extend their presence in the world.

Isn't that how we best honor the tremendous goodness of their lives?

I was to discover in a personal way a deeper appreciation for my own gift of life when, in July 2005, I faced what was for me one of the scariest, and most challenging, experiences of my life.

I had major surgery, and although the physical pain was at times the most difficult to endure, the thought that I might die or that something might go seriously wrong deeply affected me.

When I'm scared, I pray. Maybe you do, too.

When the doctor asked me about my living will the night before the surgery, I knew that a lot of extra time talking to God would be a wise use of my energy!

With some pretty intense prayer, I realized I had no choice but to radically depend on others, and especially on God. Trusting that God would watch over me, trusting in the doctor's skill, trusting in professional after-care and trusting that all of them would do what they believed was best for me became my prayer.

Prayer did bring me a certain level of confidence I had not known before. I can get through this but only if I trust that others will do their best for me, was the message I kept hearing as I prayed.

Can we really do much of anything alone, refusing to trust and rely on others, I wondered. I think not.

The close, intimate relationship of Jesus to His Father in heaven is central to the entire life of Jesus and the answer as to how He got through His own physical and emotional pain and the difficulties in His life.

With some pretty intense prayer, I realized that I needed hope. I could go through the surgery if I could muster the hope that God would watch over me and be with me during this trying time.

Hope is the strength, the ability to see more clearly, to focus more intently, on our Lord's love for us to get us through our pain, our problems, our difficulties. Hope is not the assurance that our prayer will be answered in the manner we want, but it is the strength to go forward, to see beyond, to await a brighter day ahead, despite the tremendous odds and difficulties we may be facing in the here and now.

I have always liked the saying, "Hope is the bird that sees the light and sings while the dawn is still dark."

Hope is trust in a new and brighter day even in the darkness of our lives.

Since my surgery, I've had a lot of time to reflect on what happened.

I think surgery is a kind of microcosm of life. Realizing we can't go it alone, praying for strength and trusting that others will do what is best for us, knowing that Christ experienced a similar anxiety about life and its final outcome and found tremendous consolation in His Father's goodness, were all good lessons for me to contemplate.

Sometimes, we find hope in the most unexpected ways.

My sister Muriel called, a few days before the surgery, to tell me she was going to quit her job to take care of me after the surgery.

"That would be nice," I said, "but a little radical, don't you think?"

"Well, no, I was looking for a good excuse to quit anyway and this way I'll be able to devote my full attention to you," she said.

"Okay," I thought, "whatever you say!"

I felt extremely grateful.

It was a wonderful opportunity to reconnect with her and her family.

With recovery from surgery, so with life: Love and care and kindness go a long way toward healing. The attention and care I received helped me recover physically more quickly, I'm convinced.

The only decision I had to make each day that I stayed with her and her family was what I wanted her to prepare me to eat!

My brother David drove up from Iowa as did my sister June and husband Verne. Seeing them was also a great comfort to me.

My other sisters and brother called often to check on

my recovery progress.

And like surgery, so goes life. The medical personnel were so good about stopping by to ask how I was doing, even to invite me to walk before I felt ready to do so and to administer medication.

Inviting me to walk while I was still in considerable pain and before I felt ready, that, too, seemed to be a good lesson for me to remember and apply to life.

But one question that always seemed to be on their minds, every time they came to visit: "Father, have you been able to expel gas yet?"

The question at first struck me as humorous. No one had ever asked me that before. I thought perhaps they were trying to inject some humor in what was otherwise a rather serious, melancholy, situation.

"What is this about?" I wondered, those first days after surgery.

Finally, I worked up enough nerve to ask, "Why do you keep asking if I have been able to expel gas yet?"

"Well, Father," my doctor explained, "expelling gas means that everything is working again after the anesthesia. That means you can have food again."

I'm not sure what the lesson for life there is in that. I suppose the lesson might be that we should try to keep a better sense of humor about life in general and about realizing that the most important and significant lessons of life are found in what is quite basic and simple.

And, perhaps most of all, there is a lesson in here in the importance of gratitude for the many blessings God continually bestows upon each one of us throughout our entire lives.

Chapter Fourteen:
Ten Commandments for
the Long Haul

When I was Vocation Director for the Oblates, Fr. Tom Singer, O.M.I., then Province Director of Personnel, suggested that I form a small advisory group to offer suggestions, ideas and critiques to help me and support me in this challenging ministry. I thought his idea to be a very good and helpful one.

I also thought it would be a good idea to ask Fr. Tom to present a retreat to the advisory group to help them learn more about the Oblates, our charism, our spirituality, our missionary approach. He readily agreed.

One of Fr. Tom's presentations, the last one of the retreat day in fact, was entitled, Ten Commandments for the Long Haul. He aptly described the title as "some helpful ideas to get us through life better." By "better," I suspect he meant: more realistic, spiritually healthier, greater understanding and compassion towards ourselves and others.

Father Tom unabashedly said he had pretty much stolen these ten commandments from somewhere, maybe even from several places! Just as unabashedly he told me I could use them whenever I wanted, without his permission.

I have used them often since that day.

I offer them to you and hope they are as helpful for you as they have been for me. And, please, feel free to give them to others.

I don't even care if you claim them as your own!

Please pardon the commanding nature of the verbiage. I wanted to keep them in the same tone as the originals!

Commandment I:
Thou shalt ask God to give you a "new chance" each new day. You should give others "the clean slate" that you ask God to give you each day.

Commandment II:
Thou shalt ask for a non-judgmental attitude toward others. It is God's role to judge, not yours.

Commandment III:

Thou shalt believe that an operating principle in life is that Jesus has already saved you by His cross and Resurrection. You must let others know about Christ's saving action in their lives.

Commandment IV:

Thou shalt accept that there are two important qualities for all of us to live by: being available to others and being approachable to them.

Commandment V:

Thou shalt know and understand that all of life is gift. God owes you nothing. You must realize that He has chosen to bless you abundantly, out of His love and generosity.

Commandment VI:

Thou shalt accept that you must be aware of what is a "listening heart." You must know the difference between hearing simply the words of someone and listening to their heart.

Commandment VII:

Thou shalt strive to understand others, for to understand is to stand under, which is to look up to, which is a good way to understand them.

Commandment VIII:
Thou shalt strive to value a pro-active forgiveness: to be the first one to express sorrow for any brokenness that has occurred.

Commandment IX:
Thou shalt be hospitable to others, always making them feel welcome, and at home with you.

Commandment X:
Thou shalt value the opportunity to improve yourself, whether through retreats or seminars or personal reading or walks or eating less or praying and playing more, and keep always a good sense of humor about yourself.

And, finally, some sage advice I hope I can live by and you can as well.

I believe there are three main ways to reach God in this life: prayer, laughter, and friendship. I hope you experience an abundance of all three on your life's journey.

About the Author

Father Louis Studer, O.M.I., Ph.D., is a Missionary Oblate of Mary Immaculate. He has served ten years as Director of the National Shrine of Our Lady of the Snows and eight years as Oblate Director of the Missionary Association of Mary Immaculate, the fund-raising ministry of the Oblates in Belleville, Illinois. His ministries previously have been primarily in formation ministry with seminarians for the Oblates and in vocation ministry.

Born in rural Iowa, he professed temporary vows with the Oblates in 1972 and perpetual vows in 1975. He was ordained to the priesthood in his hometown of Wesley, Iowa, in 1976.

He returns to his brother's and sister's farms in Wesley now and then to watch them "sow and reap" a rich harvest and for a practical refresher course in doing theology in rural Iowa!

Ministries:

1976-1977   Associate Pastor, St. Patrick's Parish, McCook, Nebraska

1977-1984   Teacher and Principal, St. Henry's High School Seminary, Belleville, Illinois

1984-1986   Catholic Chaplain, University of Minnesota-Duluth, Duluth, Minnesota

1986-1989   Director, Oblate College Seminary Program, Omaha, Nebraska

1989-1991   Director, Oblate College Seminary Program, St. Louis, Missouri

1991-1996   Director, Oblate Vocation Ministry, Chicago, Illinois

1996-1997   Sabbatical in Jerusalem, Israel and Cambridge, Massachusetts

1997-2007   Director, National Shrine of Our Lady of the Snows and Missionary Association of Mary Immaculate, Belleville, Illinois

Beginning July, 2007, I plan to take a six-month sabbatical of rest, prayer, visiting family and friends and a bit of theological updating.

I plan to spend sabbatical time at:

(July, 2007 — January, 2008)
The Oblate Residence
104 North Mississippi River Boulevard
St. Paul, Minnesota 55104
618-581-8858 (cell phone)

Beginning January, 2008, my address will be:

Christ the King Retreat Center
621 South First Avenue
Buffalo, Minnesota 55313-1399
763-682-1394

Fr. Louis Studer, omi